THE
WHIPPANINI
MAN

THE WHIPPANINI MAN

By C. David Priest

iUniverse, Inc.
Bloomington

The Whippanini Man

iUniverse books may be ordered through booksellers or by contacting:

iUniverse
1663 Liberty Drive
Bloomington, IN 47403
www.iuniverse.com
1-800-Authors (1-800-288-4677)

ISBN: 978-1-4759-6931-3 (sc)
ISBN: 978-1-4759-6933-7 (hc)
ISBN: 978-1-4759-6932-0 (ebk)

Library of Congress Control Number: 2012924316

Printed in the United States of America

iUniverse rev. date: 12/26/2012

PROLOGUE

All my life I've been in awe of priests . . . the dedicated and unblemished ones at least! I even believed for the longest time that they possessed some mystical power . . . and watching them from the vantage point of worship . . . on my knees in prayer . . . in front of the altar . . . I wanted to be one of them! Well . . . I made it to ordination, spent thirty years in their rank and file . . . and then came that terrible day!

I was at worship in St. Martins Episcopal Church . . . I sat near the back to accommodate my swift exit before the maddening crowd descended to say hello. Moving quietly to the side exit door, just as I always did, I heard a loud crash.

I pushed the door ajar and there . . . unfolding before me . . . was the hypothetical case that became a reality . . . A child was laying on the ground unconscious, pinned under a car. Kneeling next to the boy, balancing himself on his bicycle frame, with blood all over his shirt and hands, was a little white boy. "Help us . . . please, help my friend" he cried desperately . . . looking in my direction. The tears rolled rapidly down his face . . . his eyes bulged and the veins in his forehead stood out. I felt like he was trying to fuse me into action!

I stood frozen in the doorway! WHAT TO DO . . . WHAT SHOULD I DO! There was a tremendous shriek and a Black woman ran out into the street hysterical . . . in the middle of Lenox Avenue, Harlem . . . holding her hands on her head and screaming!

"Somebody . . . please . . . O Lord God . . . somebody please help my boy" she screamed! WHAT SHOULD I DO . . . MY GOD . . . WHAT?!

I became very nervous and agitated . . . I almost went back into the Church. Before I could get back in, the curious began to jam the exit way. They, like me, were witnesses to the horrendous scene . . . blood and carnage was all over the sidewalk.

Several elderly ladies turned to me! "Go over and pray for him Father" one urgently pleaded . . . practically taking me by the arm and leading me down the steps! "Of course . . . of course" I mumbled . . . along with some other incoherent words.

There where the fallen child lay, mangled, breathless and bloody . . . there on the battlefield of life verses death, I knelt to pray. I looked up into the clear blue sky for the words to pray . . . and I couldn't! I uttered a few words, but for the most part, my tongue was numb . . . my brain was fried . . . I had lost it!

I felt tears run down my face. "Look at father, he's moved to tears" said one of the Church ladies. But the tears were not for a dying boy . . . they were for father!

A half hour or more later, after the ambulance came and the body was pried from under the car and placed in the back, I was still there on my knees. The hysterical mother, now mentally and emotionally spent, was helped into the vehicle to be with her son. I stood up looking at the skies . . . did God take his grace from me at that moment? Had he forsaken me!? Had he taken away my gift of prayer!? Why?

All of that happened many years ago . . . but I lived, mildly tortured by the event for years!

I have retired from active ministry since then . . . and I had been promising myself a trip to Europe . . . a reprise . . . a way to celebrate and recall the vibrant years I'd spent there as soldier in the US Army!

Of all my wanderings about the continent . . . the escapades, some too tawdry to tell in polite company . . . I had loved England the best!

One day, in the autumn of '98, without promptings from anyone, I booked passage on a cruise ship (strange for me since I hate sailing) and suddenly I was there . . . unpacking my bags in a "B" class hotel off Bedford Park, London.

I decided not to waste a single day of my two week adventure, so I booked an Evans Bus Tour . . . first to Greenwich . . . then to parts unknown!

The tour began with an early English breakfast of marmalade, white tea and toast . . . and then we were off! I was sixty five years old . . . immersed in my own bonfire of the vanities, and trying to act terribly sophisticated and secure in my surroundings! The truth was, I felt more like a school boy again, off to play games. It was only my slow gait that brought the reality of my age a little closer to home!

We arrived in Greenwich to throngs of buses and tourists. I stepped off the bus and smelled the air, packed with my memories of it . . . lush and green . . . rich with history and old world drama . . . it felt good to be back.

The other tourists rushed over to the lady guide with the umbrella, while I took myself slowly over to a bench overlooking the vast expanse of the park, and sat down. I don't know when it happened but I know I fell asleep there on the bench.

I awoke very soon thereafter, to the smell of flowers . . . sweet and delicate odors. I looked directly across the wide lane for the bus which had brought me there . . . it was gone . . . so were the crowds. I was suddenly in the grip of anxiety! Had I slept too long and missed the bus back to the hotel!?

Determined to take a taxi back to London, I stood up and stretched. I looked over at the bench directly across from mine. There a young man, dressed in a dandy straw hat, white trousers and a candy cane colored coat, sitting quietly. His hair was blonde . . . so blonde it reflected the sunlight!

I sniffed the air again, looked about, and then slowly fixed my gaze upon him. I don't know what came over me . . . but I was feeling rage . . . unexplainable, undeniable rage at the sight of him! I walked quickly over to where he was, pointed a finger in his face and shouted to the top of my lungs, "You . . . Whippanini . . . stand up and fight me like a man!"

With a curious expression upon his face, the fellow looked around and then back at me (by now tears were streaming down my face and my anger was peaking).

"I beg your pardon sir, were you addressing me!?" he said quietly but fidgeting on his bench.

"You know dam well I'm addressing you . . . you punk! For years you've been haunting me . . . terrifying me! You have caused fear and dread in me for the last time! Stand up and fight me!"

My chest started to get tight, and my breathing was labored. The fury in me was causing me to faint! The sky grew darker and it spun like a top . . . I felt myself growing weak and then I blacked out.

I awoke in a London hospital with a matronly looking nurse hovering over me . . . taking my vital signs! I tried to sit up, but with a firm yet gentle push downward, she restrained me.

"There now . . . you don't want to be doing that just now Sir. The Doctor will be in to see you momentarily!" She smiled . . . it was a smile that calmed me . . . then she left the room.

I lay there, confused and wondering just what had happened! It started out as a day of fun, and I wound up in a hospital!

Just then, two persons in white hospital coats walked into my room. I recognized one to be the young man I had boldly confronted in the park. Fear instantly rekindled in me and my heart began to beat rapidly once again. The other man had salt and pepper hair, arrayed on his head as to cover the bald spots. In contrast to the younger man, he had a sunny countenance and a smile that put me at ease.

"Hello Reverend, my name is Doctor Rainford. I'm your attending physician! This is my Psychiatrist associate, Dr. Richards. It was he who happened to be in Greenwich with you when you passed out! Now, let's have a look at you shall we!?" His countenance was jolly and his manner fair . . . I trusted him!

"Have you ever been in hospital before" he said, pulling my eyelids up and down with his finger to have a look.

"Only once . . . I had double pneumonia as a child" I said.

All the while that the elder gentleman poked and prodded at me, I kept my eyes nervously on the younger man. Finally, the older doctor spoke! "Well I think you'll live" he said with a chuckle. "It must have been something that you ate. We'll take some tests to be certain however.

"I am a bit curious! Dr. Richards here told me that you thought he was somebody else . . . a person you obviously have some disliking for! That's worth looking into!

"I'm going to leave you two here for a couple a minutes while I make my rounds. You might want to talk about your episode that led to your fainting spell. I'll be back!" Before leaving, he leaned gently over me. "Just want to check your throat. Open and say ah" he said. I opened reluctantly . . . hoping my bad breath would not offend him. "That's good" he said cheerfully. He had an effervescence that won me over immediately. He turned and exited the room, leaving me alone with his colleague.

I swallowed hard and started to perspire a bit . . . then the young Doctor spoke right up! "Now you don't have to tell me anything you don't want to! I'm just here because I happened to be there when you fainted. But I'd like to help you if you think I can! Just before you fainted, you called me by a certain name! Do you recall the name and why you made an association with me?"

What could I say to him? I had no real excuse. I had behaved like a mad man!

I took another deep breath and it relaxed me! "I'm sorry about my behavior in the park Doctor. I hope you'll forgive me! I seemed to have instantly been overwhelmed by thoughts of an unhappy past . . . and a character . . . who for the most part . . . I guess . . . has been a figment of my imagination!" Dr. Richards, sat by my bed, took out his notepad and began to write.

CHAPTER 1

It had been fifty five years ago, and I still remembered it like it was yesterday . . . running out into the cold black night in my peejays. She had told me another one of her crazy stories and it scared the hell out of me. I couldn't sleep . . . I kept seeing things in the dark corners of the room! She wouldn't shut up, so I ran!

It was the winter of '47 and she, my Aunt Rosalee . . . a heavy set, thirty five year old, big boned black woman who could freeze the marrow in your bones with a look, was staying over at our house one night.

She wore ankle socks all the time and never ever let herself be seen without a head rag on! And to beat it all, she had hair on her top lip! My Grandpa, who was her stepfather, once said of her, "If ugliness was death, she'd woulda been born in a casket!"

My mother, a smart dresser, honey brown skinned woman, short, pretty . . . her half sister and younger than Roselee by nine years, was a bit of a night owl. Whenever she and her boy friend would journey to Harlem from Tuckahoe on a late date, she would ask Aunt Rosalee to babysit us. Oh joy!

I was five years old, I could remember her bad breath . . . it stank of cheap wine and cigarettes. And if we weren't asleep by the time she heard the tune The Syncopated Clock (all the TV channels went off the air then), we could definitely expect World War III was coming into the room in the person of my Auntie!

She would get mad as hell and fan our bottoms . . . and she wouldn't let us keep the light on either . . . (I was always so afraid of the dark)!

This night, my sister, my brothers and I were still wide awake. She stormed into the little bedroom where we all slept . . . four little bodies deep on a mattress . . . like sardines! And with her wine bottle in hand, she'd pull the string on the light switch . . . plunging us into utter darkness. She left the room in a huff!

We still couldn't get to sleep so my sister sang softly to us . . . songs and lullabies she had learned in second grade! Why on earth would we try a stunt like entertaining ourselves when "she who must be obeyed" told us to go to sleep, I'll never know!

She heard us singing . . . pushed the door open wide and stood there . . . framed by the door post and illuminated by the light, streaming in behind her from the kitchen! (God, she was scary!). The silhouette of her dumpy body reminded me of the Katsenjama Mama, complete with bun on the top . . . right out of the Sunday Comic strips!

"I hear ya'll in here! What the hell ya'll singin' about "she said angrily. "Didn't I tell ya'll to take yo asses to bed and go to sleep?" she roared.

My sister, who was always the brave one, spoke up . . . her voice was soft but direct!

"Aunt Roosy" . . . she called her Roosy for some strange reason . . . she always did. "Aunt Roosy . . . we can't sleep. Tell us a story please "said Diane!

There was something in the way Diane approached my aunt that softened the old gal's demeanor . . . oh, she was clever that sister of mine!

Aunt sauntered nonchalantly over to the corner then plopped herself down on the only chair in the room. Then she began to tell us the weirdest tale I'd heard to date. She took a big swig out of her bottle and broke wind before she began to speak.

"Now . . . I'm gon tell ya'll a true story! It's 'bout a shadow man we all called the Whippanini Man!" She stopped to cough one of her deep coughs. It was deep throated and nasty sounding . . .

like she had coughed up all of the miseries of the world and then swallowed them back!

I'd never remembered her not coughing . . . especially when she drank! (Grandpa said she had the consumption . . . whatever that was!).

I turned to my sister . . . "Who the hell is Whippanini Man" I whispered!? She put her finger across her lips (that was my signal to be quiet). Diane was a pro at digging at Auntie so that she almost felt compelled to open up to us . . . she played her like a piano!

Diane crinkled up the sides of her mouth. "Who is the Whippanini Man" she asked, looking innocently at Auntie! Auntie stared back at Diane . . . challengingly . . . the way she always did when she felt that Sis was trying to psyche her out!

"Shut the hell up and stop interrupting! I'm gon tell ya'll who he is" barked Aunt Rosalee, rolling her eyes between coughs. Having gained our undivided attention, she looked into each of our little faces and smiled surreptitiously.

"Now! The Whippanini Man is . . ." she stopped suddenly, looking straight at my little brother who had his hand up! Her smile had slipped away fast . . . He had just broken her mood!

"What in hell do you wont" she said pouting . . . so that she resembled a blowfish?

"Can . . . can . . . can I jes go to da bafroom first? I have ta pee" he said . . . his little eyes open wide, smiling with no front teeth and jumping up and down on one leg!

"Well . . . . go head on den! I'll wait till you git back."

I can't tell you how I hoped my brother would stay in that bathroom and never come out, just so that Auntie would get tired and leave . . . but he popped back through the door with that big funny smile on his face, as if he were anticipating the rest of the story. I had a strange feeling that I wasn't going to sleep that night . . . her stories were always so vivid and frightening!

Auntie put her grim face on. That was our warning not to interrupt her again! She began to tell the story of the Whippanini Man.

"Nah . . . yall' aint gon believe this, but he is real and he come out only at night to lil' boys and girls!" she said.

"Why only at night" said my sister. "Hesh! Let me finish the story fo you come wit the questions" snapped Auntie, wiping the neck of the bottle and taking another swig. She continued . . .

"First off, he don't always come as a man . . . sometime he come lack the sweet smell of flowers. But even when ya kaint see him, ya know it's him . . . cause he cracks dat whip an you gits dis funny feeling in yo stomach . . . jes lack you been eatin green apples!"

"Apples, who got apples?! Ken I have a apple please" said my little brother? Auntie scowled again and looked in his direction. UH OH," I thought, "HE'S GONNA GIT IT NOW!" "Shut the hell up lil boy! Aint no apples in here . . . dey's in the story!" she said.

The rest of it was about how this scary Whippanini creature got into "the guts" . . . I think that's how she put it . . . of this young boy and gradually ate his stomach out until he starved to death! I slinked down to a fetus position and pulled the cover up over my head. Somehow, I managed to fall asleep!

That was when I first saw him . . . the Whippanini Man. He was sitting on a bench in the park, and he had a big black hat on that covered up his face. His pitch black trench coat covered the rest of his body as he sat there . . . not moving . . . not an inch.

I passed slowly by the bench, trying hard not to look at his face. It was then that I noticed that I still had my Pajama's on. I wasn't afraid, at first . . . that is . . . not until he stuck his gloved hand into the air and there was a big green apple in it. He laughed and it had a ghostly sound to it. My stomach started to turn. I told myself "FEET WHEN YOU MAKE YO DEPARTURE, PLEASE DON LEAVE ME HERE!"

I started running as fast as I could. I ran and ran until I heard a voice calling my name. It seemed to be coming from the sky overhead . . . a sky that had turned an eerie pink color. Still I ran until I saw his black coat fly over my head. I dropped to the ground and crawled up into the fetus position again . . . covering my eyes. I was frightened out of my wits.

Again the voice called my name . . . Cyril . . . wake up. The ground beneath began to shake . . . like I was riding atop our old rocking horse. "Wake up . . . wake up" said the voice again. I opened my eyes slowly and I saw the welcome sight of my sister's face! "You had a nightmare" she said. Go into the kitchen and run some cold water over your face!"

I turned in the direction of the kitchen and shook my head! "Don't worry; she's drunk now and out cold! She won't bother you!"

Diane, as always, was right! I tiptoed past Auntie's cot where she was passed out! I went up to the water basin and turned the water on ever so slowly. I felt something hot and moist on my neck . . . It was her hot breath. Startled but displaying amazing control of my fear, I turned around and there she was.

"Honest . . . Auntie" I said nervously, "I just came out here to wash my face!" My lips began to tremble. I thought she was going to beat the day light out of me. Then she spoke . . . without the harshness that she was noted for . . . in a very calm voice. "What's the matter, you kaint sleep boy?"

"No Auntie . . . I had a nightmare!" I said still waiting for her dreaded left hand to strike me! Suddenly she smiled . . . there was even a tenderness in her smile. "You seen the Whippanini Man aint ya!?" How could she possibly have known about my dream?

"Come here. Let me wash yo face fo you!" I don't exactly know how it happened, but in that brief moment, for awhile at least, I lost my fear of Auntie!

CHAPTER 2

Auntie lived across the street with my Grandmother! Each morning, from her Sentinel's perch at the side window of Grandma's apartment on the third floor, she watched us go and come . . . back and forth to school!

I was full of dread whenever my mother would send me up to my Grandma's apartment. Because it meant I had to see her!

"Her" was what Auntie had degenerated to in my mind . . . similar, perhaps, to a girl bully in school whom I knew . . . Lela, by name! They both brought out the worst in me! Fear, mostly! I spent the better part of my week figuring out ways, in my imagination, to off them both!

I may have imagined it, but from the night I had my first dream of The Whippanini Man, Auntie behaved differently towards me . . . more kindly . . . even loving at times!

It was my custom to go to Grandma's house and get graham crackers and milk after school. One day I had brought my school pictures . . . newly taken by our elementary school photographer (he also doubled as the school janitor). In my concentration on the grahams and the milk, the pictures had somehow fallen out of my pocket onto the kitchen floor.

With her usual quickness, Auntee stooped down and picked them up.

"What's dis!" she said, disdainfully. I don't know why but I was trembling again . . . I always did when she spoke sharply to me.

"Oh . . . those! Uh . . . those are my pictures I took in school. The teacher told me to get Ma to buy at least one!" I looked up into her round, brown face expecting the usual scowl that was almost always planted there. Instead, it was blank . . . She stared a long time at them . . . without saying anything. And then she spoke . . . and from deep inside of her came an awful pain.

"I had a lil boy once! If he had a lived, he might look jes like you!" She said that deliberately . . . slowly! The pain seemed to have been transmitted to me . . . for it almost knocked the breath out of me! Visions of a cousin . . . long dead . . . and whom I had never seen, instantly invaded my mind!

In one of my bravest moves ever, I wrapped my arms around her, hugged her . . . burying my head into her large waist and said, "What . . . what happened to him?" She looked away and was quiet for the longest few seconds I can remember. "Whippanini got him!" Then she turned back with a sorrowful look down at me and said, "Jes like he's gonna git you!"

She took another long and thoughtful look at me, then she spoke. "You run on back over to the house! And don't you show dem pictures to nobody but yo Momma! Pichas' is personal thangs . . . sometime you flash 'em round and the wrong spirits gits em . . . bad thangs happen! Now you mind and do lik I said!" "Yes mam" I said obediently. She put her hand softly upon my head, turned and went into her room and shut the door.

CHAPTER 3

It had been three weeks since I heard the story about a cousin I had never seen and who died . . . apparently before I was born. But my mind stayed on him constantly . . . so much so that I could draw his face from my mind's eye.

I only shared my discovery with Diane . . . and no one else . . . not even my Mom! (She was too busy to listen to me for doting on her lover!). Dot said she had heard the story a long time ago!

A couple of nights went by and we all were crunched together in bed and I fell asleep last. As I got deeper into my sleep world, a distant voice kept telling me to "wake up"! It was the voice of a boy, my own voice, I thought . . . or at least it sounded to me like my voice.

I believe I had awakened, and I found myself in a row of wheat . . . golden and flowing free in the mild warm wind. I walked down a row or two and suddenly, I felt it . . . my stomach growled and I doubled over with pain. A taste came up to assault my palate . . . the taste of green apples!

As soon as I realized I was dreaming, I sought desperately to shake myself . . . to do all in my power to wake up. I looked up and the sky was a sea of blood . . . rolling over me like a river. I was trapped in dreadful dream.

I covered my face with my arm . . . shutting out the increasingly horrific scene overhead . . . red skies and blood were everywhere! I dropped my arm suddenly . . . and there he was . . . standing at the end of the row of burning wheat! There was no doubt . . . it was him . . . Whippanini!

He held out his hand to me and began to laugh . . . his laughter was raucous and like the roar of thunder. I closed my eyes and shook myself again. And as if it were magic, I was back in bed with my siblings. All memory of it was temporarily erased . . . all but the taste of green apples in my mouth.

Diane, awoke and looked at me hard. "Something is going to happen Sis . . . I just know it" I said nervously.

And then, without warning, the front door to the kitchen was hit like someone had taken a sledge hammer to it. It came crashing down . . . mother lay there on her back against the door . . . struggling with her boy friend. We all jumped up and started screaming! Lover boy had Mom by the throat and they were fighting each other like their life depended on subduing the others opponent!

Mom spit up a mouth full of blood! "Call Uncle Buck" she shouted at me! Diane rushed in and grabbed a pot . . . she hit Lover Boy with it and it slowed his momentum to a crawl! I smelled enough liquor on their breaths to start a forest fire!

Lover Boy sat there dazed . . . Mom got up, dashed to the kitchen table and pulled a knife out of the draw . . . holding him at bay with it! In the meantime, I had gotten to the phone and called my uncle, who lived just a block away. He was over to the house in a flash.

Uncle Buck was short like my Mom . . . wry, stocky and strong as an Ox. He was just back from the Korean conflict and spoiling to show Lover Boy what he learned in the jungles over there!

He saw his sister bleeding from the mouth . . . then, snarling, turned to Lover Boy calmly and said, "Oh yeah . . . hit a girl huh! Yo ass is dead meat Son!" Before anymore altercations could occur, two white cops were coming up the stairway. Their temperament was invasive . . . even before they entered the house. They even smelled menacing!

"What's the problem here" said the cop with the chevrons on is lapels.

"Officer, I want to swear out a warrant on this man! He tried to kill me in front of my kids" said Mom, holding her jaw and pointing down at Lover Boy.

"Were you two drinking . . . I mean looks and smells like you both tied one on" said the officer, facing his partner with a grin on his face. The partner had a toothpick in his mouth . . . kicking one leg of the kitchen table, pushed his police hat to the side and rested arm on the table.

"No sir . . . no sir . . . we only had one drink apiece" my mother said, trying to hold a straight face.

"What's your story" said the officer, pointing to my uncle?

Before he could answer, Lover Boy, who was still dazed from Diane's pot, spoke up. "It's a good dam thing you got here in time officer. I was just about to hurt this little runt!" . . . meaning Uncle Buck, of course!

"Oh, it's like that huh!" said Uncle Buck, snarling and arching one eyebrow! Before the cop could move an inch, Uncle had given Lover Boy a round-house to the jaw and knocked him out cold! There was the expected struggle with the cops which lasted only as long as it took uncle to lift his arms up in the surrender pose!

"Look here" said the officer to his partner "looks like a domestic thing to me! Send the kids into the other room until we get this straightened out!" he said, flipping his notebook out.

We filed past Lover Boy who was sitting up slowly recovering from Uncle's solid punch. I looked up at Uncle and softly uttered, "Way to go Unc!"

We were all huddled together in the bedroom. Diane looked at me quizzically. "I wonder if they're gonna take Uncle to jail" she said? I shrugged my shoulders! Then I turned to her and said, "You see Sis . . . I told you something bad was gonna happen! I taste them green apples!"

CHAPTER 4

That night was etched forever in my memory. The police didn't prefer charges against my Uncle, (they claimed he had provocation for his actions) . . . my mother dropped the charges on Lover Boy and . . . three weeks later, they were back at it . . . bar hopping . . . go figure!

Ten years had passed. Mother had slowed down a bit and was even content to stay at home more often. Diane had formed a girl singing group that was doing surprisingly well . . . they were booked for Amateur Night at the Apollo Theater in Harlem!

Things were looking up and I hadn't dreamed of or given any thought to Whippanini in years . . . he and Aunties stories seemed at last like a figment of my childhood imagination.

One hot summer's night, Mom had to work late . . . I found myself at home with my younger brother. My sister had gotten dolled up for her big night at the Apollo. I went to bed early only to be awakened by a knock at the door. It was a buddy of mine named Nicky!

Nicky was my idol . . . suave, sophisticated, and from White Plains. His claim to fame was a car which the young ladies loved to ride in. He was nineteen and a teen heart throb. Looks wise, he was a poor man's Johnny Mathis . . . without the crooning ability!

I opened the door and he stood there holding on to the doorpost. His eyes rolled a bit in his head. I could tell he was inebriated. Although I was a bit unsure, I asked him to come in! I offered him a glass of water. He declined and in his slurred speech offered me a ride in his car.

"Come on Cyril. I know you don't want to be stuck up in this hot house. We'll take a run over to Yonkers and be back before you know it."

I would normally jump at an invitation to go riding around in Nicky's car . . . it was a Chevy with shiny chrome on it. The girls always swooned when they saw us in it.

But for some odd reason, it struck me that I should not take up his invitation! "No thanks Nicky, old pal. I've got to stay here and watch the house till Mom gets home". I somehow knew he wasn't going to let me off the hook that easily.

"Come on! My boy Tanky is sitting in the car now waiting for us! We're always a barrel of fun when we hang out . . . you know that! Come on!" He added a further enticement, "If you come I'll tell Tanky to sit in the back and you can ride shotgun!"

Seconds later, there was another knock at the door and it opened. Auntie was standing there, surprisingly well dressed and without her usual head rag, but looking suspicious. "Is yo Momma home boy" she said . . . looking over my shoulder at the kitchen.

"No Auntie, she's working late".

"You watching the house" she said, looking Nicky . . . wickedly eyeballing him.

"Yes Mam! I sure am!", I said, clearing my voice slightly.

"Well! See that you do jes' that!" said Auntie firmly. In her signature style, she sniffed the air over Nicky's head, scowled and went back out of the door.

"You see Nick, I gotta stay" I pleaded.

My younger brother Ken, who had been watching TV in the living room, suddenly popped up by my side. He had been quietly listening to our conversation.

"Can I go Nicky . . . please" he said . . . with eyes wide open in anticipation of a yes? Nick looked a bit disappointed, but said yes. They both left and I went to bed again.

I lay there seeking the comfort of sleep for an hour, but was restless! I got up, opened my homework assignment and rechecked it. Not even that made me sleepy so I turned the TV on. That seemed to do the trick as I remembered nothing more until I awoke to the front door slamming!

Mom had come home tired and hungry! She was irritated. It seems that Lover Boy didn't show at her job to pick her up and bring her home.

"Where are the other kids?" she asked. Before I could get an answer out, Diane came running up the porch steps and through the door . . . grinning from ear to ear. "We got second prize at the Amateur Show" she said, in the most excited voice she could muster! Mom smiled and hugged her.

Suddenly my mind began to tune out . . . and I didn't know why! It was as if I was all alone in the house. I looked around at the four walls and saw the flowers in the wall paper . . . they looked real almost! Then I could smell them . . . they were expelling a fragrance . . . sweet and pungent! For no apparent reason, fear to gripped my heart! My belly began to ache!

I could hear more footsteps coming up the stairs . . . then a knock at the screen door. I heard my Mom say, "Come in officer!" The word officer made my heart beat faster! I raced into the kitchen to see what the matter was. I recognized him . . . It was Officer Satch.

"Hello there, Mrs. Willis. I don't want to alarm you but I have to inform you that your son Keith was in a car accident tonight with two other boys on the New Jersey Turnpike and . . ." Mom screeched out a frightening sound . . . Dot quickly held her tightly around her shoulders . . . I felt weak in the knees!

"Hold on . . . now . . . hold on, before you get yourself all excited . . . he seems to be Ok! He's at Lawrence Hospital and he's being checked out."

"Oh . . . . thank God . . . thank God" said Mom, heaving a huge sigh!

"I gotta tell you though" said Satch haltingly, "the other kid died. He was on the passenger side and was killed instantly!"

Stark fear and then a loathing came over me . . . loathing for me . . . my inaction! NEW JERSEY TURNPIKE . . . HE SAID

THEY WERE GOING TO YONKERS . . . I mumbled to myself!
I could have . . . I should have stopped Nicky from leaving! He was
too drunk to drive and I knew it. Worse than that, I had let my
brother go with him! Suppose . . . !

I held my hand over my mouth . . . turned and walked slowly
back into the living room. Officer Satch's words were muffled from
then on. I heard him say that the driver was alright, ". . . just a few
bruises" he said.

Tanky sat where I should have been! Nicky was alright! As if I
were choking, I pushed my stomach in . . . and out came a belching
sound from my mouth. The after taste was that of apples . . . green
apples!

I had a loathing for my life in that small village! I swore to do
everything in my power to leave it, and the memory of all who lived
there and touched my life in such painful ways . . . to leave them
all behind. At the moment of my resolve, I promised God I would
never have any children . . . none to bring into a world of pain and
misery as I had been.

CHAPTER 5

I stopped talking to take a drink of the cold water that the nurse had brought to me. Along with it, were some sweet pears . . . from the can of course! I looked at them! They looked like apple slices! I suddenly lost my appetite!

Dr. Richards had his face buried in some notes . . . looking them up and down . . . mumbling softly to himself!

"Have you ever spoken of your childhood experiences with anyone else . . . like a teacher or another psychiatrist" he said? I took another swig of water and gave a deep sigh. "Not really! My sister has been like my psychiatrist . . . she's the only one I've ever really talked to about it."

Before another word was spoken between us, Dr. Rainford came back into the room. "Sorry it took so long! Well, I'll tell you what's going to happen. We have found a clot over your lung area! I've got you scheduled for an EKG and a cardiogram. That's for today. Tomorrow you'll undergo a battery of other smaller tests! The clot may have been the reason you passed out . . . but, as I said, the tests will give us more information."

The two doctors simultaneously looked at the clock on the wall. "Why don't you and I go get a cup of tea and let this poor chap rest a bit before they come at him" said Rainford? I smiled . . . hoping it would hide my concern for what I had just heard! They left and while I shuddered to know the truth of my health problem, I felt secure in the confines of the hospital . . . I was getting care . . . and thoughts of Whippanini were beginning to fade once more!

It was the end of the week and my dismissal from the hospital was at hand! The results of all the tests were in and all I could think of was getting back home to the good old USA. I awaited the final review visit of Dr. Rainford! He came into my room with a display of energy that seemed, at least to me, to be his hallmark.

. He sat by my side and grabbed my upper arm. "You're not going to like this but I'm going to have to keep you another week!"

"Another week! But you said I could leave tomorrow!" I shouted, nearly jumping out of the bed!

"Now, now hear me out!" he said, calmly! "I believe we've found the source of your fainting spells . . . you, my friend, have developed a pulmonary embolism!"

"A What" I shouted angrily!

"In Laymen's terms . . . a blood clot attacked your lungs! We think it began in you left leg and worked its way up to your lung!"

I eased my body back onto the bed and began to collect myself. Rainford reached over for my arm grabbed it firmly and pushed my shirt up. He wrapped the band around it, inserted the stethoscope into the sleeve and began to take my pressure!

"Another week!" I mumbled, looking away from him . . . thoroughly disgusted.

"Shhh!" he said, squinting his eyes to read the pressure gage.

"Your pressure is up a bit . . . we've got to get it down to a normal place. You've got to avoid getting anxiety over this little set back. We're going to give you heparin and wean you slowly onto wayfarin. You should be good to go by the end of the week! In the meantime, get some rest! Dr. Richards will be in to see you momentarily!" he said as he exited!

"I hope his got better news than you just brought" I yelled at his back! WHERE IS THE MONEY COMING FROM TO PAY THIS HOSPITAL . . . I asked myself! I'LL BE DAM NEAR BANKRUPT BY THE TIME I GET OUT OF HERE!

A few minutes later, Richards came in! Before he could say good morning, I assailed him. "I don't want to stay here another week!" He smiled broadly!

"I see Dr. Rainford has given you the bad news!"

"You darn right he did . . . and I'm upset by it!"

"Maybe, you'll feel a bit better if I tell you what I've found out!"

My curiosity kicked in . . . and remembering what Dr. Rainford said about my blood pressure, I struggled to remain calm. I became almost placid! It was as if he had a potion to relieve me of my anxiety! "Go ahead Doc!" I entreated him.

"Well, it's just this! I checked out some documents in the archieves of our National Museum. It seems that some Cajun people immigrated to England during the French and Indian War. They came here to escape religious persecution . . . to England of all places!

It appears that they were a part of a small cult which sprang up in one of the poorest parishes in the City of New Orleans! At the center of their religion was this character . . . a kind of Court Jester! They called him the Whip Man! Did you ever hear that name mentioned when you were a youngster?"

"No . . . I never had!" I said.

"There's more! This Whip character used to carry a whip with razor sharp silver spurs at the tip of it. He would use a poisonous snake and a child . . . the human sacrifice, in his ritual service. He'd put the infant in a trance and then lay it naked in front of the snake and his followers would begin to make low, mournful sounds to entice the snake to strike at the child.

Just before it struck out . . . to show that he was merciful . . . the Whip Man would take his whip out and lash the snake . . . cutting it to pieces until it was dead! He'd then bring the child out of the trance and . . . get this . . . he'd give the child a green apple!" Dr. Richards leaned forward, staring up at me for my reaction!

"My God" I said! What a way to get stupid people to follow you!" Richards continued:

"It seems he did more than that! He got filthy rich from the monies that came in from his congregation . . . there were wealthy

English people in the Cult as well. All of the survivors of the snake ritual became his wards . . . more like his slaves! That's how much influence he exercised over them. The government here finally outlawed the cult . . . oh about 1920."

I sat back down slowly on the bed, turning over on my side to face the doctor. I glanced up at the ceiling and back. "But how did my Aunt come to know this story" I said, almost whispering my question.

"That's the mystery! The only thing that I can tell you is . . . one of his main rules for all the women in his cult, was that they had to wear head scarves . . . or some other kind of banding around their hair!"

I stood up on my feet again . . . pacing nervously and wringing my hands . . . I didn't know why! It was puzzlement to me. "I still don't get it! Where would my Aunt have gotten such a story!? She's not from New Orleans. Our family, on my Grandmother's side, was from Virginia", I said emphatically!

"Did your Aunt have a friend . . . or someone she may have associated with . . . who was from New Orleans" said Dr. Richards?

"No one that I know of" I said! Richards snapped his fingers, making a loud cracking sound! "Wait one minute! In your story, didn't you say that your Auntie had a child that died!?"

"Yes . . . a boy cousin that was still born" I said. As I spoke I fell deep into my own thoughts.

"Is your Aunt still alive"? Richards's curiosity furled his brow with his question. I responded a bit bewildered.

"No . . . no she's not! She died in 1980!"

There was a moment or two of silence between us. I didn't know where he was leading me with his questions! His next statement quickly cleared the air for me. "If you're wondering why I'm asking these questions, it's because I believe that there is something or someone in your past which is causing you to manifest this character . . . to bring him into the reality of your conscious world. Your Aunt may be the connection here! If we can find the origins of this, I believe it will help you get rid of Whippanini once and for all!"

CHAPTER 6

Later that evening, my ever competent, always pleasant night nurse came in with a bag of heparin which she hung up on my pole. Then she injected the lead into the I V tubing . . . turned on my night light and left the room . . . smiling benignly as always!

The rest of the night I spent tossing from side to side in my bed . . . more than a little depressed! I searched in my heart and head for clues. Was Dr. Richards right!? Could I be going mad . . . or was I somehow adding a kind of strange psychic power to a myth . . . the memory of which had been with me since childhood!?

I remained secluded in my room! About late evening, I got up to go to the bathroom. To my surprise and utter discomfort, the door was jammed . . . no matter how hard I yanked on the lever, it just would not open.

Grabbing my I V pole firmly, I hurried out of the door, down the long corridor and into the ward bathroom. As I passed by, I noticed that the night light was on at the desk but there were no nurses assistants anywhere around.

I got to the bathroom and it was unoccupied! What a relief! I no sooner began relieving myself when suddenly, the lights went out . . . plunging me into total darkness. I panicked for a second . . . I could hear my heartbeat. STAY CALM . . . REMEMBER WHAT THE DOCTOR SAID ABOUT YOUR PRESSURE!

And then the scent filled the room . . . flowers . . . potent and aromatic . . . making me dizzy. My whole body trembled and I

21

slumped down onto the cold floor and began taking exaggerated breaths.

I dialogued with myself . . . desperately seeking self control! "Breathe in slowly . . . let it out slowly . . . keep calm . . . this is a hospital, for crying out loud . . . the lights should come on automatically! But, maybe the generator blew! Come on . . . keep breathing! Oh God . . . my God . . . let this not be Whippanini again!"

A mysterious light filtered through the ceiling. There, on the plastered wall in front of me appeared a hole . . . it was like a worm hole, only smaller . . . eating its way through to the black of night outside! My eyes popped and my jaw clung open . . . was I going insane? I felt something wet on my leg. I pissed myself!

Images began to form . . . human images. There upon the wall were the likenesses of my Auntie and my Mom! They were in a barroom together. My Aunt was visibly upset and snapping at my Mom. "Aint you comin' home to them kids! I got's to go to work . . . I can't stay with 'em all day!"

"How did you find me" my Mom asked . . . her speech was slurred . . . she had been drinking a lot!

"Don' be stupid! It's the only bar in town fo us colored folks . . . where else you gonna be?"

"I'm not leaving here till he comes back!" Mom said.

"Well then, you gonna be here all night long. I jes seen Lover Boy drive off with Margarie!" Mom's face dropped and she began to cry . . . her mounding was the sound of personal defeat!"

Teardrops streamed uncontrollably down my cheeks. I stuck both hands out . . . trying in vain to touch the face before me "Mommy . . . mommy . . . don't! I love you . . . you don't need him" I shouted!

My Aunt stormed out of the bar . . . angry and disgusted. Just outside, standing at the stop sign was a man . . . a fancy Dan type of guy . . . in a brown pinstriped suit with an Ivory walking cane. He tipped his derby hat to Auntie, who made moves to get around him. "Hi you doin' Ms Rosalie . . . you memba me don't ya? I was to yo birthday party bout ten years ago. Gilkes Anderson, at yo service"

He smiled widely at her . . . his mouth was filled with gold fillings and there was a magic twinkle in his eye!

I realized, at that moment, that I was seeing visions of the past! All too quickly the scene changed to my Mother's deathbed, thirty years later. Auntie had already died and Mom was all that was left of the Old Ones! My greatest joy in life was to see the gleam on her face when, years before, I become an Anglican priest!

I knelt there beside her bed in prayer, as if I was at the altar. She raised her hand slowly and put it on my face . . . stroking it very gently. "Mom, everything is going to be alright! You'll come out of this and . . ." I started crying before I could even finish my line! With a halted breath, she spoke. "I want you to take care of things when I'm gone" she said slowly.

"But Mommy, you aren't going anywhere" I insisted holding tightly to her hand.

"Oh yes . . . yes I am! But I'm not fearful son . . . I've lived my life, you know! Whatever God intends for me is alright . . . I'm satisfied with whatever judgment he has made. I deserve it!" She looked up at the ceiling overhead. Her eyelids flickered like a butterfly's wings . . . her eyes rolled around as if she were watching something. Again she looked at me!

"How can you say that? I mean you're a good woman! God is going to reward you when you get to heaven . . . I just know it!"

"Is that the truth Father, or is that just wishful thinking . . . or do your own fears tell you that your old Mom may not be alright!?"

Her breath was leaving her . . . I started to cry again.

"Look son! You have to overcome your fears in life like I had to overcome mine! You know, when you live your life full of fear, you reap a fearful reward. Look at me in my later life . . . I went to Church every Sunday . . . lived a Christian life at the last . . . not because I loved God, but because I was fearful of his judgment! Going to Church every week don't matter if you are just going through the routine. So many folks goin to hell . . . just on they way to heaven!"

A sharp pain seized her body and she squeezed my hand hard. "I don't have much mo time son! There's something I put off tellin' you that I have to tell you now" said Mom in almost a whisper!

The pain struck her again. This time she waved her to arms in front of her face as if she were terrified . . . as if she were warding something off.

I panicked and immediately ran out to the Kitchen and got her nurse. The nurse looked at her then dashed to the phone and called an ambulance. "What . . . what's happening" I yelled at the top of my lungs? "She's having a stroke . . . this one is big" said the breathless nurse!

By the time the ambulance arrived, my mother was gone! I stood by the window crying . . . watching helplessly as they loaded her corpse into the back of the vehicle and drove off. The Nurse brought me some tea and tried to console me. I didn't hear a word that she said . . . I was numb all over . . . I felt like a plant that had been plucked up from its roots . . . I was now a motherless child!

The scene suddenly disappeared. I closed my eyes and pinched myself. WHY AM I RELIVING THIS . . . WHY!? I opened them again and he was standing there where the images had been. "Ha ha ha! Did she tell you anything" said Whippanini! I looked on him with fear mixed with disgust.

"If I could, I would kill you!" I said, gritting my teeth.

"Hahaha. I'm sure you would. But indulge me for a moment . . . did she tell you?" I didn't bother to answer the loathsome creature!

"Well . . . I'll just have to keep coming back until you find out the truth . . . now won't I? Hahahahahaa!" He vanished before my eyes!

I heard footsteps coming down the corridor towards the bathroom. The door swung open slowly and rested against my thigh. It was my ward Nurse and Dr. Rainford! He knelt down and took my pulse. "I thought something was amiss when I couldn't find you in your bed!" he said.

Suddenly the lights came on! "I'll help him back to the room Doctor" said the Nurse! "You'll do no such thing! You'll run and get a wheelchair this instant. I don't want him walking back on his own!"

CHAPTER 7

It was exactly one week later when my release order came. I was ecstatic to be leaving the hospital, but a little reluctant to give up the excellent care I had received under Drs. Rainford and Richards.

The latter didn't even blink when I told him about the bizarre events that took place in the corridor bathroom during the blackout. He told me of his intentions to search around until he found some evidence that my visions and the story my Aunt had passed on to me, were somehow linked to the cult of Cajuns who had long ago come to his country.

My whole vacation had thus far been spent cooped up in a hospital bed . . . chasing a figment of my imagination! With the time I had left, I was going to make the best of things and see the English countryside.

The legendary London rains began . . . torrents of water splashed against my windowpane. I stared out at the city . . . watching it become drenched . . . hypnotized by the raindrops and grateful for the peace that it conjured up in me.

The phone rang . . . shocking me at first. I picked it up cautiously. That moment I felt as if I were in a Hitchcock movie! It was Dr. Richards. "Old man, I know you'll be checking out of the hospital today. If you've got the time, is it possible you can meet me someplace!?"

"Sure thing Doc! Where do you want to meet up?"

"There's a local pub in Paddington. They call it the Bull n Bear.

It's right across the street from St. Mary's Church . . . not hard to find at all!"

"What time do you want me there?"

"If you take the tube to Paddington Square in an hour, you can be there by 2pm. Will that be alright!? In fact I'll meet you at the exit from the train!"

"See you there at 2pm. Thanks Doc!"

I found the station tube easy enough. All the way to Paddington, I sat in deep thought. I wondered what Dr. Richards had found out . . . and if I was about to discover the root causes of my mystical and terrifying adventure. What if what he found only served to make matters worse! I couldn't bear that thought at all!

The train came to a stop at my exit and I got off! True to his word, Richards was at the top of the exit way stairs . . . waiting to greet me.

"What's this all about" I asked, hurriedly shaking his hand!

"You need to see this!" he said.

"See what?"

"I was having a beer in the Pub when I came across a tapestry. It tells a story of the Cajuns I told you about! Apparently . . . many of them settled right here in this town!"

"You're serious", I said a bit incredulously!

"Of course am! Come see for yourself. It's hanging there still!" said Richards, pulling gently at my elbow . . . leading me on!

Once inside, we both sat down for a moment! Doc stepped to the bar and ordered two pints of beer . . . we sat there and drank. All the while we kept looking at the many art hangings and splendid painted glass windows with medieval themes etched in them.

My eye caught a lone tapestry! It hung on a wall close to the dart board. I went over to get a glimpse of it. There were remarkably vivid images of Black people . . . men and women in period costume . . . dancing around a chair . . . with a roaring fire in the background. There, In the foreground, like he was guarding them all was a man with a cane . . . and ivory cane. Bug eyed, I came back to the table and sat down. "See what I mean" said Richards?

Looking over to the bar, Richards spotted someone.

"Wait here a minute . . . I'll be right back" he said.

He brought back with him a tall square jawed, cockney speaking gentleman . . . a classic Dickensonesq looking character with great bushy eyebrows and a broken nose, who was one of the bar attendants.

"Reverend Sir, this is Mr. Everett Bottoms. He works the bar here and is its 'sometime' local historian" said Doc.

"Pleased to meet ya" said Bottoms, rubbing his hand on his apron and then extending it to me . . . flashing a big smile. I shook it and smiled nervously back at him.

Doctor Richards invited him to sit down with us. He lowered his head slightly then spoke to the man.

"Tell him what you told me a little earlier this afternoon!" said Richards . . . soto voce!

"This afternoon" the man said, speaking loudly, scratching his head to jar his memory?

"Yes! You know . . . about those eh . . . . !"

"Oh yes, them . . . them unmentionable people!" said he, winking his eye to let us know he had caught on!

"When I was a lil nipper, I used to be in the Sunday school . . . right across the street there at St. Mary's parish. The Vicar's wife was me teacher. We had this kid in the class . . . black kid . . . who was always asking her questions about the Holy Ghost . . . nuthin else but that! When she tried her best to explain it to him . . . he told her that he had seen him. He told her that the Holy Ghost appeared almost every night at his house in the cellar!" The bar attendant then gave me a long stare . . . he knew he had my attention!

"Get to the part where you and your buds stole into the lad's house one night!" said Doc . . . you could see the excitement in his face! I nervously took a big gulp of beer. The attendant continued.

"Well, that was a helluva night, I can tell you! Me and my mates . . . Sunday school chums . . . well, we decides to pay him a visit to his house after dark . . . you know, jes jokin round!

We goes up to this deserted barn on Taliston Hill Road where they was living. We sneaks upon the rooftop . . . nice n easy . . . we peeps through the window light and that's when we seen it!"

"See . . . eh . . . saw what" I said, thoroughly engrossed in his story?

"The whole lot of 'em . . . Black men, women and children . . . chantin' and swaying back n forth . . . kneelin round a chair. It looked like it was some kinda throne . . . sittin up high . . . it was! And in the chair was this man . . . he was glowin' with a long black cloak on and long stringy white hair. He was holding that kid in his arms like he could crush him to death . . . and the kid was sleepin' . . . least ways that's what it looked like ta me!"

"He could have been in a trance" said Doctor Richards . . . thinking out loud and looking straight at me!

"Whippanini!" I told myself. "Go on . . . go on" I insisted.

"Well that was all there was to it! Me mates got spooked and we all ran like the dickens back to town! The next day, we told the town folks how we saw zombies back there at the barn!"

CHAPTER 8

Doc Richards and I took the Tube back to London proper and he invited me to dine with him at the fabled Kingsley Cauvery. I sat at table . . . across from him . . . silent and brooding . . . feeling strange and not my sometimes jolly self! I didn't want to pursue the matter further . . . I really wanted to get on with plans to see the rest of England in the remaining four days until my ship sailed home.

Sensing my reticence, he reached out and placed his hand on my shoulder.

"Look old man, if you're not up to this, I can call a halt to . . ." I didn't want to appear like a coward . . . so I cut him short!

"No, no! I'm just a little bit tired today . . . that's all! I guess it's old age catching up with me!" I managed to put on yet another fake smile.

The waiter came with our food. I took a bite or two and then put my fork slowly down onto my plate. I looked into the Doctor's eyes, "What's wrong with me Doctor . . . why am I going through this bizarre experience at this point in my life?"

Through the window I could see that the daylight had nearly vanished over the horizon . . . the restaurant grew dim and our waiter lit the candle on our table . . . an accommodation for people who like ambience, I supposed. I suddenly grew cold and numb . . . the way I always did when I didn't really want an answer to my question.

"I really can't say" said Richards, with compassion in his voice that made me think that he was really thinking it through!

"There are many experiences which shape our lives as children . . . they linger on, like ghosts, to sometimes affect the actions we take. Call it fate, call it whatever, something in your past has lingered with you long enough to make you have this great fear of it. Just when you think you have mastered it, it manifests itself again . . . and this time it's manifested itself . . . to you . . . in human form!" He paused to let it sink into my mind!

"Let me suggest something else. I had planned to go out to that old Barn tomorrow and have a look around! The Barkeeper you met promised to introduce me to the Parish Vicar. I want to ask the Reverend a question or two . . . but if I discover that your Aunt or any other relative of yours is remotely involved, I wouldn't have a clue, without you there, as to how to connect the dots!"

I picked my head up . . . smiled again, this time a little more convincingly. "What the heck. If it's only one more day, how can that hurt" I said.

"Good! I'll meet you at the same spot at the same time tomorrow!" He hoisted his wine glass up in the air. "Here's to you and solving this mystery!"

A good meal, a few glasses of wine, and a raucous joke or two . . . courtesy of the Doctor's rich British humor, lifted me from the doldrums. We spent hours there. We laughed all the way to the front door where we bid each other good night.

The night air was fresh and had the nippiness of autumn . . . that change of season that had become, for me, reminiscent of the good days when I used to vacation here.

My hotel was just a few blocks away from the Cauvery . . . there wasn't any need for a taxi . . . so I walked the streets of London . . . taking in the scenery with its row houses, shiny brass door knobs and brick chimneys dotting the skyline. The streets were well lit . . . I felt safe.

From my vantage point, just a few blocks away, I could see the British Museum . . . it was always my marker . . . I knew I wasn't far from the hotel.

I passed an Anglican Church . . . old and majestic looking with spires that reached into the sky. The full moon with its' radiant luster shone bright . . . so bright that it lit up the church roof so that I could even see the shingles.

I stopped in my tracks and stared up at the roof. . . were my eyes deceiving me or were there silhouettes of children running along the gutters on top? I yelled up at them "Boys . . . boys, come down from there. You'll hurt yourselves!"

One of the rough and toughs in the group screamed back at me, "Who the hell are you! It's none of your business we're up here!"

"Come down this instant" I insisted! "I happen to be a Priest in this Church and I'll call the Coppers if you don't!"

Without another word, the two big toughs scampered to the drain pipe and slid down to the sidewalk! As they ran away, I heard one yell "Gudbye Black Jesus". They quickly vanished. Taking no offense at them, I even laughed a bit!

Once more I looked up and there was one lone, slight of build boy, shorter than the others, clinging to a loose pipe fitting! I couldn't see his face . . . I could barely make his form out against the moonlight.

"Can you get down to the ground by yourself son!?" I said.

"No sir" replied a feeble voice. I could barely hear him but I could tell he was afraid!

"Stay there . . . I'll come and help you!" YOU'LL BE LUCKY, YOU OLD FART, IF YOU DON'T BREAK YOUR OWN NECK . . . I told myself.

Divine mercy came to our aid as a stranger . . . a young, strongly built lad, was walking by. I hailed him and told him of the potentially dangerous situation and entreated him to help the boy to get down. He did so gladly. "You don't want to climb roofs this time of night . . . you might hurt yourself!" he warned the boy. With that, he placed the lads hand in mine, tipped his hat and went on his way.

My instinct told me to locate a constable . . . to leave the boy with him and get back to the hotel. There was something compelling about him, however! He couldn't have been more than eight years old.

I could see he was cold and a bit disoriented. "Can I take you to the tube or something"? He didn't speak . . . just shook his head no . . . not looking once into my face. "Are you homeless", I said? Again he just shook his head, indicating he wasn't. "Are you here with your mother or father?" There was more silence and a vacant stare! "Well . . . are you hungry"!? It was then that face lit up . . . he shook his head again . . . this time it was a yes!

NOW YOU'VE DONE IT . . . THE BOY'S HUNGRY . . . WHERE ARE YOU GOING TO TAKE HIM THIS TIME OF NIGHT? My first thought was to go back to the Caurvery! "But how would that look? How will you explain this scruffy boy . . . at this time of night . . . to the personnel who just waited on you!" Difficult indeed!

LOOK! TAKE THIS BOY TO THE POLICE STATION AND HAVE DONE WITH IT! My rationale, which was good most of the time, failed me.

I recalled a little pan cake house in Chelsea! "I'll bet . . . (bending down to get a closer look at him) . . . I'll bet you could use some pancakes and syrup just about now." I could see by the instant gleam in his eye that he was up for that!

I hailed a taxi, which stopped on a dime. "Take us to MY OLD DUTCH on High Holborn . . . the one in Chelsea" I said snappily. "Right you are sir!" The boy and I got in and we were off.

It was just a few stop lights before the driver, who had been keeping a suspicious eye on the boy and me through the rear view mirror . . . spoke.

"Kinda nippy tonight hey Gov'" he said cheerfully.

"Yes, it is a bit nippy" I said half heartedly . . . hoping that would be the end of his questions.

"That your boy there "he said?

"I beg your pardon" I said, assertively!

"I mean . . . he looks like ya! Spittin image" he said.(The kid didn't look like me at all!) I smiled sharply at him turning my head to look out at the passing traffic . . . end of conversation for my part!

Our taxi came to a stop right in front of the restaurant! The driver called the fare out . . . and as I felt about my person for my money clip, he put on a big smile . . . as if he sensed his tip might be in jeopardy! "I din't mean to pry back there Gov! But ya know how it is nowadays . . . ya got to protect the young ones, what runs the streets at night from all kinds of strange people. But then, it aint none o my business!" OH GOD, DID HE JUST MAKE IT CLEAR WHAT WAS ON HIS MIND!?

CHAPTER 9

The atmosphere inside the restaurant was warm and inviting, and the smells delicious . . . like a candy shop without the candy! A windmill replica was on display along with big colorful balloon cut outs . . . dotting each wall . . . and the shelves were lined with big Dutch platters . . . adding to its already rustic atmosphere.

I led him to a big chair, which confirmed my initial thought that he was indeed just a little boy . . . for once in it; his feet didn't touch the floor! I sat next to him and that is when I noticed . . . his hair was coarse and curly . . . he wasn't white, but a mulatto.

For fear of extending myself to him beyond politeness, I quickly stuck a menu into his hands. He turned it one way and then the next. MAYBE HE CAN'T READ, I thought. "Here, let me have that!" I said softly. I pointed to a picture of crepe's with scoops of different flavored ice creams. "Do you think you could go for that" I said? He looked up into my face, smiled, exposing his missing front teeth as he shook his head yes.

The waitress came to the table to take the order. "Bring us one order of those delicious looking crepes . . . for the boy here. I'll just have coffee thanks" I said.

The service was surprisingly swift . . . our order was on the table in minutes. During the meal, I thought to myself, much of what passes for genuine gratitude in life is not articulated at all, but often can be read on the face and in the eyes of the recipient.

As he ate his food, I realized he was really hungry and that he was thanking me, and conveying it with those magnificent saucer brown eyes and big bites of food. I found myself wanting to find out more about him, but . . . no . . . DON'T EXTEND YOURSELF!

"How about some more syrup for those pancakes son" I said? He nodded his consent, chewing fast, and kicking his little legs under the table. It didn't take a mind reader to know he was happy . . . at least for the moment!

Attempting to help himself, he placed his rather small hands, which were now greasy, around the large glass of water. As he lifted it to his mouth, it began, slowly, to slide out of his hands.

"Here . . . let me help you with that" I said. I held on tightly to the glass while he drank. As he drank, I could hear him making gulping sounds with his throat! He was soon finished.

"Thank you" he said softly . . . pinching his mouth closed to chew on a tiny piece of sausage! THERE WE GO . . . BESIDES HIS SOFT CRY ON THE CHURCH ROOF . . . THOSE ARE HIS FIRST WORDS TO ME . . . NOW WE'RE GETTING SOMEWHERE!

"You really are a polite young man" I said, sincerely. His smile was his currency . . . I was captivated by the innocence of it.

"Tell me, how did you get up on that roof tonight" I said? And then, with a look of uncertainty which very few children can disguise, he turned away briefly, but kept on chewing and kicking his legs.

"I mean . . . it's alright of course if you really wanted to be up there!" I said coyly. He waited a couple a seconds more, then he spoke again.

"It was Roger and Finley's idea. They made me go with them!"

"Roger and Finley . . . hmm! Well are they your family?"

"No sir . . . they live in the same town as me!"

"Where is that?"

"I'm from Paddington". I stalled for a moment . . . there was that town again!

"I'm really . . . really from Shepherds Bush . . . but the Constables took me to Paddington to live when my dad died."

"How did your Dad die, may I ask?"

"He was murdered!" He kept kicking his legs and eating as if he had said nothing of consequence. My mouth opened but nothing came right away. "I'm sorry to hear that" I said, recovering my composure moments later.

"Some bad men waited in an alley for him and beat him up! They stole his paycheck and left him there!" said the little boy.

"Well then, is your mother still with you" I said, hoping to change the subject!?

"No! They said she drank a lot and couldn't take care of me. So they came and got me and took me to Paddington to live at a shelter!"

My brain was spinning again! I WONDER IF THIS BOY COULD HE BE A LINK TO THAT CULT THAT THE BARKEEPER TOLD US ABOUT! I remained unflustered and calm.

"Since I fed you real good tonight, would you mind telling me what your name is" I said? He looked uncertain again. "You're not going to say Oliver Twist, are you?" I laughed to put him at ease.

"My name's Huck" he said proudly. HUCK! NOW THAT BEATS ALL . . . but this was a little boy after all, and the hour was growing late . . . my questions would have to wait!

"Ok Huck! I'm going to take you to the tube, and give you some money for the fare back to Paddington!" I leaned over the table and smiled at him.

"Don't you want to come with me!" said Huck in a voice which sounded almost like a desperate plea! His little lips began to tremble. There was a fear in his face that was indiscernible.

"Ok, I'll tell you what. Suppose I ride with you to the Paddington stop! Will that make you feel better" I said? Again he had lost his tongue and gone back to shaking his head.

He finished eating as I stared at my cold cup of coffee, called for the bill, bought him yet another ice cream . . . in a cone, and we were on our way to the tubes.

We walked slowly and I watched him twist and roll the cone to catch each melting drop of ice cream. I wasn't aware of when he did it, but quietly, he had slipped his hand into mine as we were walking.

He had made a little mess of himself with the ice-cream. I took out my handkerchief and slowly wiped his mouth . . . It gave me, at that moment, the allusion that he needed me. There was a lump in my throat . . . the moment was so powerful it brought tears to my eyes! "Are you alright mister?" he said casually, still licking his cone.

"Oh yes . . . I'm just fine" I said, gently squeezing his little hand.

We boarded the Tube and headed for Paddington. He had finished his ice cream and was beginning to nod . . . sleep was finally intervening in our new relationship. His head eased gently onto my arm . . . blessed sleep rescued us both!

At the station stop, I woke him up. We got to the top of the exit stairs and I bid him goodnight! "Well Huck . . . here we are my boy! Can you make it from here?" I said. In character, he shook his head in the affirmative. "Put it there pal" I said, extending my hand . . . he shook it in a comic and warmly exaggerated way.

The fact that he was leaving filled me with melancholy. He took as few steps in the direction of the shadowy street before us. Then suddenly, as an afterthought, he ran the few steps back to me, motioned with his finger that I should bend down to him. I bent over . . . he threw his little arms around my head and kissed me on the cheek! "Thank you for the ice cream Mister . . . nobody ever bought me an ice cream before".

He skipped off down the street and out of sight . . . the stubborn tears remained on my eyelids as I watched him disappear. I pressed my cheek gently with my fingers.

CHAPTER 10

The train pulled up at my station and I ascended the stairs onto the streets. A local clock near a telephone booth was striking twelve o'clock pm.

I walked briskly in the direction of my hotel. All the while my mind was on little Huck! I felt fearless and free somehow . . . he had done more for me than I for him. I never had a child of my own and now . . . now I was feeling this pressing urge to be a father . . . to replace the one that he had lost.

I fought back the urge to go back . . . to find his shelter . . . to see him again. I could even imagine going through adoption procedures for him . . . so much had he touched my heart in so short a space of time. But there was that voice screaming in my head again . . . YOU SENTIMENTAL OLD FOOL . . . DON'T EXTEND YOURSELF . . . YOU'LL GET INTO TROUBLE!

Before I could even notice it, I had walked the distance back to the Museum. I paused there to think . . . to clear my mind of the evening's events.

Suddenly I looked up to the top step. There was a man . . . twirling an elongated object and whistling . . . standing with his one leg against a huge pillar. He had a derby hat on, a pin stripped suit, and spats, shining like florescent bulbs, on his shoes. My imaginings overtook my reason as he pointed the object at me . . . like his spats, it too began to glow! "Hey there! Aint you Ms. Rosalee boy" he said . . . his booming voice filling the air.

Without hesitation, I turned and walked as fast as I could in the direction of my hotel. With every step I took, I could hear equal steps matching mine on the pavement behind me. There was no one else around . . . my heartbeat quickened . . . my pulse beat so loud, I could hear it! I dared not turn and look for fear that there was someone . . . something behind me!

The park entrance gate was open . . . I could see my hotel dead ahead. I turned into the park and began to pick up my pace . . . huffing and perspiring as I went!

Then, as suddenly as they started, the ghostly footsteps were hushed. I could only hear my own. I was halfway through the park when I slowed my pace to a halt and, in dread fear looked slowly behind me. My starker was gone.

I breathed a sigh and turned back in the direction of the hotel. YOU'VE GOT TO STOP THIS BOOGIE MAN CRAP AND GET A HOLD ON YOURSELF! I moved with dispatch until I was inside the lobby . . . safe!

I must have looked like death warmed over from my experience. The Bell Hop at the desk had to speak to me more than once before I understood that he was inquiring after my health! "Are you alright sir" he asked? There is no way I was going to admit to him that I had just . . . possibly . . . just possibly seen a ghost!

"Oh! I'm fine" I said, still a bit shaken. "I just walked a bit too fast for my age" I said, brushing the whole thing off.

"There's a gentleman waiting to see you sir" he said.

"A gentleman . . . waits for me? Who is it and where is he" I said?

"He's sitting in the lounge there. He's been here for the past hour!" I careened my neck to look into the lounge but saw no one.

"I'll go and have a look" I said.

I walked into the very posh and delicately decorated room . . . with replicas of late nineteenth century furniture. Seated in an antique Saint Ann's chair was Dr. Richards . . . fast asleep! I had him in mind as I came into the Hotel and his appearance there was, to me, a God sent. I shook him gently to wake him. He jumped slightly being momentarily startled.

"Oh it's you! Did they tell you that I found your wallet", he said, wiping his face with one hand?

"My wallet"!? I reached into my walking jacket and indeed it was gone.

"Yes! You left it on the table at the Cauvery! You got away before they could find you. They know me and so they gave it to me to give to you! So old man, here it is" he said handing me my wallet. Out of habit, I looked inside.

"Oh it's all there, I assure you! I only pick your pocket when I send my bill to you"! He laughed heartily . . . I managed a grin.

He yawned and stretched a bit, looking somewhat weary. I wanted to slow him down . . . to tell him about little Huck . . . to make him listen to my latest distress. But even to me it all sounded like the ravings of a person who was about to have a mental breakdown.

"I'll be off to my own world now" he said. I shook his hand and asked my question of the evening . . . more to stall than anything else. I didn't want to be alone just now!

"Off to your wife, I suppose "I said, baiting him on.

"Me, married? My goodness no! Not yet anyways!" An impish smile flashed on his face. I rambled on . . . concerned only to have someone to talk to just now . . . before facing the challenge of being up in my room alone.

"I'm not married either! I think . . . do you think . . . I mean . . . is it possible that not having that aspect in my life is unsettling to me now!" He arched his eyebrow . . . as if he was confused.

"Hasn't that . . . I mean . . . when people . . . when people find that out, don't they . . ." I fought valiantly to get my point across to him.

"Do they sometimes give you a wide berth . . . is that what you' asking!?"

"Yes! Yes, that's it!"

"Oh God yes! It's a sign of the times! Mention that you're unmarried and some people hit the reject button . . . especially if you're a professional person. They begin seeing you as the other . . . somehow incomplete. Immediately, they get a mental process going in their heads, which encases you in a box . . . and the box is over a trap door which opens up and down you go . . . free falling externally into an abyss!" He laughed!

"My heavens . . . that's vivid!"

"What do you expect . . . I'm a shrink after all?" He winked his eye and smiled . . . then he became reflective. "But as for you my friend . . . you have to deal with the fact that your fear . . . whatever it may be . . . has temporarily taken hold of you! You're not crazy . . . you just need to deal with this . . . look your demon square in the face and spit at him!"

"I wish it were as easy as that", I said.

"Are you ready for tomorrow". I shook my head.

"Then I'll see you in Paddington. Good night Rev" he said. He took his leave of me and I went to my room.

CHAPTER 11

Sticking my key card into the slot, I opened the door slowly to let the light from the hallway filter into the room. I turned the lights on. I was freighted beyond reason but, my fears were soon abated. The room appeared clear of all hob goblins, ghosts and things that go bump in the night!

I sat on the freshly made bed, staring up at the ceiling . . . contemplating the prospect of easing into the covers and getting a peaceful sleep. DON'T FOOL YOURSELF . . . THERE'S NO PLACE WHERE HE CAN'T GET AT YOU! My mind was not going to let me sleep. I kicked off my shoes and rubbed my feet . . . got up and went into the bathroom.

At the moment when calm began to displace fear, the lights in my room started to flicker! My immediate reaction was to panic. ITS HIM . . . I KNOW ITS HIM! Just as quickly it stopped! GET A HOLD OF YOURSELF! Then I saw something, like a shadow, flash past the closet door! THAT WAS NOT MY IMAGINATION! SOMETHING IS IN MY ROOM . . . CALM YOURSELF . . . CALM YOURSELF . . . YOU DON'T SMELL GREEN APPLES!

I took a deep breath, stood up straight then walked confidently out of the bathroom into the hallway. Once there, the lights flickered again. When they stopped, there in front of me was that man I saw on the steps of the museum . . . sitting in my comfort chair . . .

slapping the palm of his hand with the knob of his ivory white cane.

"Come in . . . come in here Ms. Roosy boy! Don't be afraid" said the man in the chair. His grin and those teeth with the gold caps left no doubt . . . he was the man in the pin stripe suit . . . the one I dreamt about when I was a child.

"Who are you . . . how . . . how did you get in here "I said frantically . . . backing to the door? His laughter mocked me!

I ran to the door . . . yanked at the lever but the door wouldn't open. He sat grinning and rubbing the knob on his cane . . . looking at me as if he were my jailor. I dropped to my knees, closed my eyes and clasp my hands together in prayer.

"Oh here comes the priest now hey!? Good . . . I a priest too" he said facetiously. I opened my eyes slowly . . . my whole body was shaking.

"Oh I don't stand in no pulpit and preach . . . or say a lot a mumbo jumbo around no altar table . . . but I'm a priest jus da same! You gonna see how good I am soon . . . I gonna dance and sing for you! You like dat?" he said.

I clinched my hands all the tighter. My determination was to get them out . . . get the words out! OUR FATHER, WHO . . . WHO ART IN . . . . CAN'T THINK . . . I MUST THINK!

"Hey, you finish!? Good! I'll tell you why the words . . . dey don't come out . . . the prayer that is! Because we took it from you! Oh yeah! Whip Man and me . . . we took it from you." He pointed his cane towards the ceiling. "He aint gonna hep you no more! Don't believe me . . . try to pray . . . right now . . . go ahead" he said defiantly. He stood up, spread his legs and laughed.

He was right and I knew it . . . I really couldn't pray . . . I would think the words but they wouldn't come out! I was mentally tired and soon resigned myself to whatever fate he would have prescribed for me.

My head got hot . . . so hot It felt as if my brain was frying. I started to reel and faint . . . but I managed somehow to keep hold on my consciousness. "Who are you . . . what do you want from me" I shouted?

"Me? Hmph! I don matter so much . . . but I work for the Whip Man! He wants you . . . real bad!" His emphasized the "real bad" part.

"What!" I said, still dazed.

"He want you boy! You escape him for the last time. It be a full moon soon boy . . . now he catch up with you and gonna take his prize!"

"What prize!? I'm no prize" I said, still shouting! "What does he want with me?" I could hardly speak for trembling.

"Remember when you was a lil baby boy . . . back when you was sick with the pneumonia! Well yo momma put you in the hospital . . . thinkin you was gonna die! Whip Man come for you and you wasn't there. Somebody pull a switch and he took the wrong baby boy!"

"What are you talking about" I said, licking my perspiration off my lips.

"Ms Roosy! Dat gal pull a fast one! She knows what the Whip Man can do! So she take her baby, whats already dead, and put him in the hospital crib. Whip Man come and take him and you . . . well you escape. You escape again when you was suppose to go on dat car ride . . . memba that . . . but the other boy he take instead of you! You escape, escape, escape . . . until now!" He laughed and snarled his upper lip.

My strength had dried up! I looked over by the edge of the bed. The room service hadn't taken away the cart from breakfast. IF I COULD ONLY . . . SHOVE IT AT THE DOOR . . . MAYBE SOMEONE WILL HEAR IT!

I shoved it with all my might! It stopped just short! The Cajan Man looked at me and snarled again . . . then raising his cane over his head as if to strike me, he moved in my direction. The door opened and a young man with a hotel uniform stood in the doorway!

"Sorry sir! Hope I didn't frighten you! I didn't know you were here. I came to pick up the tray from this morning's room service!" said the young man servant.

I looked at the chair where my adversary had sat . . . he had completely disappeared. Only the echo of his laughter remained for

me to hear. I felt like Scrooge spared of his last ghostly apparition . . .
completely humbled and drained of energy. The man servant noticed
me still on my knees.

"Are you alright sir? Can I help you get up!" he said politely.

"Yes . . . yes you can" I said.

He gave me his arm and I pulled myself to my feet and sat me
on my bed. "Shall I call for the doctor sir" he said?

"No . . . no! I'll be alright" I said.

In that instant I had a flashback! I saw the young man who had
helped me with Huck . . . I saw his face clearly . . . more clearly than
I had at the time he had offered his help.

"Don't I know you" I said?

"I don't know sir" he said.

"Didn't we meet earlier . . . tonight . . . on the street? Were you
the young man that helped save the boy up on the Church roof
tonight" I said. As the memory of that moment hit me, my life's
energy began to resurface.

"Now that I recall it, I suppose that was me sir!" he said with a
gentle smile. "Will that be all Sir" he said?

"Yes . . . and thank you . . . for everything".

"No problem sir" he said preparing to leave with his cart.

"Oh . . . just a minute . . . just a minute more" I said loudly,
reaching for my money clip.

"Yes sir" he said.

I had a twenty pound note . . . all that was left of the change in
my pocket! I handed it to him with a grateful heart!

"Oh no Sir . . . that's not at all necessary" he said, vigorously
waving his hand over the money! "Good night sir!" he said.

My savior was gone! I stared at the door a long time after he
existed, summoning up courage to turn around and face the chair
again. My ghost like character was also gone. I pulled back the
covers on the bed, got in . . . fully clothed . . . and had a peaceful . . .
nightmare free sleep!

CHAPTER 12

The afternoon train was packed with riders . . . of every hue and color . . . shoppers with bags and with personal computers . . . many just standing with earphones in their ears . . . tuning out the world! WHAT UNCOMPLICATED LIVES THEY MUST LIVE . . . WOULDN'T IT BE SIMPLE TO TUNE OUT MY WORLD . . . RIGHT ABOUT NOW! "I wish I were one of you" I whispered under my breath.

Like clockwork, Richard's and the Barkeeper met me at the Paddington exit. We went immediately to the Church. Richard's rang the doorbell to the Rectory and a stately, well dressed, handsome Black woman came to the door. She opened it.

"Can I help you gentlemen" she said.

I noticed the shabbiness of the entrance way . . . the broken screens and the peeling paint. It was an old building . . . being made much more so by obvious deferred maintenance. As a cleric I despaired to see it . . . HOW COULD THE VICAR ALLOW FOR THIS?

"Yes. My name is Dr. Richards. This is Reverend Williams, and I believe you know Mr. Bottoms here . . . our local eh historian!" (I nodded my head . . . acknowledging the lady's presence.)

"Yes I do. What can I help you with gentlemen" she said?

"We're here to see your husband mam!" said Dr. Richards.

"My . . . husband!?" she said, with a vague expression on her face.

"Yes Mam . . . the Vicar" said Richards.

"I'm am the Vicar" she said!

Both Richards and I looked at each other then at Bottoms . . . who stood there embarrassed, shrugging his shoulders!

"Please excuse our ignorance Vicar . . . some of us men are still dealing with our ridiculously high testosterone levels" said he.

"It's quite alright; I'm used to it by now. Come in gentlemen"

The Vicar made us comfortable; then she went into her modest kitchen and put a kettle on. Richards whispered in my ear, "Let me do the talking at first" he said. I nodded in agreement. She came back, sat down, and without a word, cued us with a look.

"I know you must be very busy Mam, and so I will come right to the point. We're doing some research on cult groups and we've heard there's a group here which may help us with our research. You a have some Black Cajans from America who, a half century or more, once settled here in this village and lived in this very house, do you not?" said Richards.

"Yes . . . We have rather extensive records of their activities here in the parish" she said.

"Would you mind sharing those with us" he said!?

"No . . . Not at all! I'll tell you what all I know about them . . . the rest you can take from the records! First and foremost, they were treated badly on the basis of race from the moment they arrived. People called them darkies and a cult. And while they did develop some backward Christian practices . . . baptizing animals and the like . . . they were generally harmless and peace loving people.

The children even went to Sunday school here. There are a few of them who still come down, occasionally, from the old Taliston Hill farmhouse where they have lived for decades. If you'll wait one minute, I have a scrap book with some pictures of them. I bring it straight away to you" she said.

Being in that house and hearing what she was saying about the cult was beginning to challenge me in ways I did not want Richards to know. THIS IS NO MYTH! THIS SO CALLED CULT ACTUALLY EXISTS. I then wondered if my family could possibly be linked to it! NO . . . NO . . . IT'S NOT POSSIBLE! But how did Auntie know the legend of the Whip Man so well?" I wondered!

The Vicar Lady came back with a rather large journal book in her hands. She sat down with it . . . opened it slowly and began to educate us about them.

She told us that they were a group who respected their woman folk highly . . . blended Christianity with the practice of worshipping their household gods and ancestors.

"They were not welcomed in the Parish because some of them would dance down the aisle, "during solemn Evensong" she exclaimed, ". . . and chant their own chants and sing their own songs. The disruptions became intolerable . . . so much so that the Bishop of the Diocese, after complaint from the Vicar, ordered them removed. It was then that they pooled their meager resources to buy the old vacant barn house and were said to have "secret and demonic" services there" she said.

She sat the book between us so that we could read the fine script under the light. There were pictures of some of the older generation of cultists. My eyes zoomed in on one man . . . a young man . . . in a brown suit. My anxiety was nearly bubbling over . . . although I made every effort not to show it. I pointed to his picture.

"Who's that?" I said coyly . . . taking my handkerchief out and wiping my face of nervous perspiration.

"That is the leader of the group . . . for close to seventy years he was their guide and ruler. Their people said he was more like a voodoo priest!" she said.

"What was his name?" I said.

"Martin . . . Martin Anderson. He went back to America and took a wife! He brought her back with him (There was an instant lump in my throat and I began to stare into space). She continued, "I believe his nickname was Jilkes . . . at least that's what everyone called him."

The screech of the kettle interrupted her. "If you'll excuse me a moment gentlemen, I'll get your tea!" she said graciously. Her steps were unnerving as she stirred about the kitchen . . . her heels bumping the tile floor.

"I thought I was to do the talking" said Richards softly. I ignored him respectfully and continued to direct my questions to the Vicar as she moved about.

"This . . . this Jilkes fellow . . . did he have a cane?" I said.

"She stopped instantly in front of the kitchen entrance and gave a peculiar look.

"Yes . . . an ivory cane. But how did you know that!? (I smiled but remained silent on the issue).

"He went everywhere with that stick. He was arrested once for abusing one of the children with it. He nearly beat the poor child to death! One of his own members reported him for it . . . the group was down on that sort of thing where their children were concerned. Turns out it was his own wife who reported him. Seems he struck her with it as well . . . she was rumored to be pregnant at the time of the assault! She sought refuge from the local constable!" she said.

Dr. Richards turned to me . . . he had an awareness on his face that told me that this was what we were searching for.

"Do you have a picture of her as well?" I said.

"Oh yes . . . just one second more!" she said. She came out with a tray of biscuits and hot tea and placed it down in the middle of the table. "Now . . . let me see!" she said, leafing through the pages.

"Here! Here she is . . . this is her" she said emphatically. I gazed at the picture and was stunned. I stood up and walked slowly over to the window and looked out.

"Is there anything wrong Reverend" asked the Vicar?

"No" I replied . . . my guts roiling, "Nothing at all!" The picture was of Auntie as a young woman . . . I'd have known her anywhere.

I could tell that Dr. Richards suspected I was hiding something. He cast another glance at me and I could feel his psychic energy hitting my brain like so many arrows. He continued now with his own questions.

"Vicar, we've heard that they perform rituals of some sort. In the Tavern there's a tapestry which tells the legend of the group. (Bottoms remained quiet but nodded his head vigorously).

"On it they dance and wear period dress . . . they have a huge fire in the fireplace and they dance around a chair in the middle of the room. Have you ever witnessed such a thing" he asked her?

"My God yes . . . my Grandmother used to belong to the group . . . that is until she was able, through a good family here in town, to get a job and work her way out of it. For awhile I was a child of the group. We danced and sang until midnight . . . always at the full moon. At one point the elders only were permitted to be in the Common room. They were waiting!" she said.

"Waiting!? Waiting for what?" said Dr. Richards.

"Waiting for one they called the Whip Man! I never saw him myself . . . but they always brought a male child in with them."

"Why a male child"? I said, suddenly involved in the conversation again.

"Because that was tradition . . . the presence of a male child was supposed to entice the Whip Man to come. They believed that he would come and take the child . . . as a gift!"

"Did he take the child . . . did you ever see the child again "I said?

"As I said . . . I never entered the room when they called for the Whip Man in their ritual. The group believed, in order to survive in this new country, they had to keep the custom of providing a male child to be chastised by the Whip Man . . . like in the slavery days in America. The child was to undergo a ritual cleansing . . . in this case, a whipping" said the Vicar.

"But did the child ever rejoin the community again" I said desperately. There Vicar sat down slowly.

"That was the strange part. Every boy child that participated in the ritual was never seen again. We were told by Jilkes that he put the child up for adoption!" Suddenly it dawned on me to ask about Huck.

"Do you . . . did you ever hear the name Huck before" I said?

Her eyes lit up again as before . . . there was excitement in her face.

"Do you know Huck . . . He's one of the mulatto children in my class . . . bright little fellow! Poor dear . . . I'm told he spends more time in the box than in public!" she said in a musing voice.

"In the box!" I shouted, my curiosity full blown!

"Yes! That's where they put the children who keep wandering about or just plain run away!" she said. "Has he run away . . . is that how you know him" she said?

"No . . . No" I said.

"Well, do you mind if I ask how you do know of him". She was persistent in her questioning.

"It's just that I ran into some boys near my hotel who were being a bit truant the other night. One of them said his name was Huck and he was from around here" I said, hoping my explanation would suffice.

"He's also up at the community . . . it's a shelter for children you know! The authorities took him there when his father died!" she said. I dropped quietly onto my chair and sighed! "Huck . . . Huck"!

Richards stood up and began to pace about the room. He turned suddenly to the Vicar.

"Vicar, isn't tomorrow night a full moon"?

"I believe it is!"

"Will there, most likely be a ceremony . . . will the group have a dance then" he said!

"Yes! But if you're thinking about going up there to watch them, you will probably find them most inhospitable . . . they don't like intruders!" she said.

"We don't mind that, do we men" he said boldly, turning to me. "How's about it old man . . . can you endure another day!? We may find the truth of this yet" he said boldly!

"Yes . . . yes! I've come too far with this to turn back" I said.

"Tomorrow being Sunday and all, If you come around early in the morning, you can do Mass for us Father! It would be a treat for some folk to have a male on the altar!"

"I'll try . . . I'll try" I said!

"Now there's a challenge" said Dr. Richards, looking intensely at me.

CHAPTER 13

I returned to my hotel . . . tired, frustrated, and a bit hungry. I hadn't eaten any of the tea and biscuits the Vicar had offered. Instead I rang up the hotel room service and ordered a light snack.

The rain had begun to fall . . . a heavy mist settled over the city of London . . . the air had lost that nippy quality I loved and it was getting outright cold!

A vacation in England was to have been a respite for me . . . it was becoming a drudgery . . . I was losing what was left of it and my edge on sanity at the same time!

Still there were those redeeming moments . . . dealing with and trying to overcome ancient fears, and of course, meeting Huck! My mind continued to drift back onto him . . . even as I dealt with past ghosts and Whippanini!

Huck represented for me innocence . . . pure innocence that must be protected! The thought of a little boy like him being locked up in a box was unnerving . . . I wanted to do something about it . . . but what!?

There was a gentle knock at the door. With trepidation I got up from my chair to answer it! I opened it and to my delight, it was the same bellhop who had brought my meals twice before . . . who had saved little Huck from the Church roof! There was something reassuring about the lad . . . something that fortified me and made me less stressful and forlorn . . . making me all but forget about the events of the past two weeks.

With a quiet but congenial smile, he rolled the food cart into the room. Maybe he was some other personality; altogether different from my impressions of him, but for that moment . . . for my drastic need to feel stable . . . or just to have a human being around me . . . he fit the bill perfectly.

With a panache that was even entertaining, he pulled the lid off the food, and pointed to it with his finger. With style, he opened my soda bottle with a firm twist of the cap . . . then pointed to the condiments on the tray and smiled again. "Is there anything else I can help you with sir!" he said.

I thought for a second or more. "Yes . . . yes there is" I said. You can tell me why the world is such a hard place for a child to grow up in?" I could tell by his facial expression that I had taken him totally by surprise. "Well, the Lord did say 'suffer the little children' "he said convincingly.

I continued my dialogue; more as my attempt to delay him from leaving than anything else . . . I needed human contact just now!

"Did you have it easy when you were a youngster" I said, sitting down on the bed and poking the napkin into my shirt.

"I beg your pardon Sir" he said! I could tell the question caught him slightly off guard.

"Your life as a child . . . what would you say it was like" I said?

"Well sir . . . I led a somewhat quiet life" he said humbly, folding his hand together behind his back. He gave me a hesitant smile again. "If I may sir . . . why do you ask" he said"

"Just curious . . . I'm thinking right now about my own life as a youngster . . . how some of the events of it, may well have complicated things for me in my later years!" I stuffed some bits of food into my mouth in order to give him a chance to respond. He took his time and responded thoughtfully.

"I'm not sure just what you expect me to say sir" he said!

"Say whatever you like! Say . . . the truth of your life! I need to hear some truth right about now!" I said.

"Well sir . . . where should I start!? My life so far, on the whole, has been uncomplicated! I have lived a regimented existence following my father's orders to the letter. I took this job because it allowed me not to think too much for myself . . . not to get ahead of him and his plans for our family." He stopped there. His brow furled and he looked pensive!

"Well go on! Surely you must have had moments when you strayed from his plan . . . didn't you want to start a family for yourself!?" Again his head dropped gently to his chin . . . then rose again to look at me.

"There was a girl . . . a beautiful girl from Camden" he said. Again he was quiet.

"Well . . . what happened did you court her?" I said enthusiastically . . . hoping he would open up!

"She . . . rejected me" he said softly . . . his demeanor was sad now!

"What about your Father . . . does he live close by?"

"No sir . . . he lives in Scotland . . . with the rest of my family"

"Oh, so you're Scottish!" He had a big smile on his face.

"Oh yes Sir!" he said proudly.

"Well . . . I guess I'm happy that somebody is happy tonight "I said, taking a sip of my soda.

"Sir, do you mind me saying something" he said?

"No . . . not at all. I'm rather enjoying our conversation" I said.

"You seem to be unhappy! I don't quite know why I feel that . . . I did the last time I came to bring your snack as well! I can feel it . . . almost like there's heaviness in the room with you!" he said. I was suddenly and easily dumbfounded now . . . I could never respond to sympathy or understanding with unemotional detachment . . . OH BOY, HERE WE GO AGAIN. PLEASE DON'T LET ME CRY INFRONT OF HIM!

I lowered my head now! "I've been going through some fearful times since coming here to England" I began to confess to him like I was talking to a priest.

I can't remember all that I said to him! Just before leaving my room he turned to me and said "I don't know what I can say to help you Sir. This much I do know . . . you have got to face your demons!

I'm young but even I know that. If you don't your fear of them will eat you up and make you angry all your life. My father used to say, 'When you're angry, you wither on the vine and die"'. He was right of course . . . but then he always is!" I wiped my fallen tears away and touched his arm.

"Do you think that I'm withered and dried up of life" I said.?

"Only you can answer that Sir! I just hope you find the courage to face what is making you unhappy. If you do, then you can live better!" OUT OF THE MOUTHS OF BABES! He turned to go!

"Can I get you something else before leaving Sir?" His words had soothed me . . . his wisdom was profound!

"No . . . my boy! I think you've done just enough for now!" I said.

He left . . . and this time the echo of his voice rang in my ears, ". . . He did say, suffer the little children . . .".

In hope of a peaceful sleep, I put the TV on! I lay in bed watching . . . hoping it would keep me company until sweet rest came. The BBC was airing an old re-run of memorable moments at The Last Night of The Proms. The haunting melody of Blake's Jerusalem struck a forceful yet hopeful note in my soul:

> "Bring me my spears of burning gold . . .
>   bring me my arrows of desire.
> Bring me shield, O clouds unfold . . .
>   bring me my chariot of fire.
> I will not cease from mental fight . . .
>   nor shall my sword sleep in my hand.
> Till we have built Jerusalem . . .
>   in England's green and pleasant land."

I could not know what the next day would bring . . . but the heavy cloud of fear and foreboding was somehow lifted from me. Like a gift from above, sleep settled in . . . my rest was a grace from God!

CHAPTER 14

The next morning, Richards met me in the lounge of my hotel. We had breakfast and, afterwards, went straight to the tubes and headed for Paddington.

We arrived unceremoniously at the Vicar's doorstep. She was arrayed in a cassock, preparing for service.

"Come in gentleman!" she said warmly. "I hope you are going to grace us with your presence on the Altar this morning Father!" She said! I looked sheepishly at Richards who turned conveniently away!

"Yes . . . yes of course! I'm honored by your request" I said.

"That's great. Directly after service, I'll take you up to the Taliston Hill compound so that you may visit with little Huck!"

My eyes lit up and I became almost jubilant! "That would . . . that would be very nice indeed" I said chokingly.

Once in the sacristy, I robed in priestly garments and processed into the sanctuary, being led by the procession of acolytes, choir and the Vicar. She preached a wonderful sermon and all proceeded according to the specified liturgy of the Anglican Church . . . that is . . . until the time for benediction.

I stood before the altar of God as the Celebrant . . . before the people of God . . . opened my mouth . . . and nothing came out! Anderson's claim reverberated in my head, ". . . Whip Man and me . . . we stole ya words man"! For seconds on end I tried and tried, but still no words of benediction came forth.

The people in the front pews looked at each other . . . totally astonished at what they were watching! And then, as if I were being reprieved, I heard the words from the Vicar's mouth, "The grace of Our Lord Jesus Christ, the Love of God, and the fellowship of the Holy Spirit be with us now and always . . . Amen". She had rescued me!

The recessional hymn began and we went back into the Sacristy. Inside the little space, the Vicar said the final prayer. I disrobed in the quietude of the moment . . . feeling lost, alone and unworthy. She walked up to me and placed her hand gently on my shoulder, "You are not the only person to experience a crisis of faith!" she said softly. I looked into her face . . . the warmth and understanding there said it all! She had insight!

"Do you suppose that's what it is" I retorted, with a smirk!

"I know it when I hear it dear brother! I also know the cure for it as well" she said, looking me straight in the eyes!

"Tell me . . . for I truly would like to know" I said!

"Engage! Engage your fears, and the word will return to you"!

She pressed my shoulder gently, and went to her office.

The Vicar, Dr. Richards and I walked the quarter of a mile up to Taliston. There, at the top of the hill stood this large, imposing and somewhat forbidden looking barn house. The Vicar led the way to the entrance and wrapped soundly on the door. A pleasant and radiant faced young black woman answered and bid us all come in. We told her that we were there to see Huck!

"Huck is on punishment right now, but I can let you see him for a moment or two, and talk with him if you like!" she said politely.

"We would like that very much" I said eagerly!

She escorted us into a larger room where some youngsters were playing games and preparing their lessons. Their manner seemed exuberant . . . It was hardly what I expected to see . . . the children . . . all smiling and having fun.

She then took us to the room called THE BOX. "Here is where we put those youngsters, especially young boys, who have a problem associating properly with the other children.

She opened the door slowly and we entered. There were three boys in the room doing various things. Light streamed through the windows illuminating colorful paintings and art, obviously done by children. It was a pleasant change to what I had expected!

The young woman called out his name. "Huck, there are some people here to see you". From the furthest corner, the little figure of a boy emerged . . . the sunlight shown on his face. It was him alright . . . Huck . . . just as I had remembered him.

He looked up and pointed to my face. "It's him . . . the ice-cream man. You see . . . I told you . . . I told you he'd come back for me" he said, looking intently up into the young woman's face. My emotions ran the gambit from being overjoyed to being overwhelmed. Either way I was so glad to see him again.

The Vicar stood there smiling, while Dr. Richards had a confused look on his face. Suddenly the little boy came up to me and put his hand in mine. "Are you going to take me out of here and be my Dad" he said. It was as if he were reading my heart and mind. I had no idea why this child should affect me so.

"Would you like me to do that" I said?

"Yes I would like that. I could have ice cream all the time then!" he said. I laughed raucously . . . my heart was full.

"Well not all the time . . . sometimes "I said, trying to communicate how much it meant to me to be there with him . . . in my smile.

"You know that it's not impossible for you to adopt him. I'm one of the Town Registrars and I sit on the adoption board. If these good people here are willing . . ." the Vicar was politely interrupted by the young female attendant!

"I'm not at liberty to make decisions! If you want I'll have our Curator get in touch with you!" she said nervously.

"Curator!? I hadn't heard of that before! Who holds that post" said the Vicar?

"Why, Mr. Anderson does . . . he always has been" she said! Both the Vicar and I turned to each other and exchanged curious glances.

"Would it be possible to take Huck down into town for the day" I asked?

"I could let you use the parish hall for a brief visit . . . a little time to get to know one another!" We all began walking back to the parlor. The Vicar turned to the young attendant again, "Would that be all right!" The young lady became visibly nervous and was awkward in her speech!

"I . . . I . . . I don't know . . . Well . . . if you . . . if you come back later perhaps . . . maybe!" she said.

Just then the door opened forcefully and my mouth did as well. For standing in the doorway was the man in the pin striped suit . . . the one I had seen in my room! It was impossible; I told myself . . . my heart was racing with feelings of anxiety again.

"Who are these people" he said coldly and callously! The young woman stood there stymied . . . her lips trembling.

"Who let the boy out of the Box" he said, rolling his eyes menacingly in the young woman's direction.

"I'm . . . I'm sorry sir! These good people from the town asked to see him" she mumbled.

"Well . . . send him right back . . . now!" he said sternly, placing his cane across his shoulders . . . assuming a threatening stance. The young woman took Huck immediately by the hand and back into the box. The Vicar spoke up, "Now see here Sir, we didn't come here to start any trouble, we just wanted to see the boy".

Anderson brushed his sleeve with his hand. "No problem at all Vicar Lady. I'm sorry to be coarse in me behavior . . . but it's me job to be protecting each and every child here. I be sure you understands that!" he said, smiling . . . showing his bright gold teeth.

"Can we take the boy to the village for a visit . . . we won't keep him long" she said. Anderson sucked his teeth and walked slowly around us in a complete circle. He seemed resistant to the idea.

"Tell you what! Tonight we having a big celebration here. You all are welcome to come. Why we don't put the visit off til then!" he said, smiling that uncomfortable smile again.

"We'll . . . we'll be happy to come back for your festivities" said Dr. Richards, winking one eye at me to go along with his suggestion.

"Yall be here at eleven oclock then! Till then, I have to begin me preparations . . . tonight is gonna be a big night for us!" he said, looking directly at me.

CHAPTER 15

Like an expectant father waiting for his child to be born, I moved up
and down in the Vicar's living room. She busied herself by preparing
tea and other treats for us. "Just a little something to hold us until
later" she said, sitting down next to me.

Richard's cell phone rang and suddenly, he took his leave of
us . . . he had to get back to the hospital. He explained that they had
summoned him on emergency and that he would be back before we
left for Taliston Hill. "I wouldn't miss this gathering for the world"
he said reassuringly. As he walked out of the door, my heart sank!

The hours ticked away and I was becoming more and more
apprehensive. I had taken an uneasy nap on the Vicar's couch, but it
was in no way refreshing for me. Soon she came into the parlor and
spoke to me! "It is now ten o'clock and Dr. Richards isn't here yet! I
suggest that we go up there in about one half hour . . . I'm sure he
will meet us there" she said confidently!

Somehow, I felt alone in this endeavor . . . my mind told me
that no matter what, I have to be there for Huck!

In the meantime, the Vicar poured tea and kept me company. I
thought about how relaxed I was with her.

"You make some spot on tea!" I said! She smiled, blew on her
cup and took a sip.

"I can also make a mean pot of stew!" she said, not too shy!

"Is that an offer?" I said . . . amazed at how forward I was
becoming with her.

"Only if we can get through this, and you bring the wine!" she said.

I sat there in silence, sipping my tea. Occasionally I would look at her out of the corner of my eye. She was indeed a good looker for her age (I guessed she was fifty or so). She was the first woman clergy I ever saw who wore earrings and lip stick during Evensong! I liked that! She suggested that we remain in our cassocks for the trip up to the Barn house.

The old parlor clock sounded the chime for the half hour. I stood up and stretched nervously. "Well, I guess it's about that time" I said!

"By the way, what is your name . . . may I ask" I said!

"It's Vicar!" she laughed. "No its not . . . it's Connie!"

"I'll go bring the car around" she said.

We arrived there at the stroke of eleven. From the car we heard voices singing accapella . . . melodies that were pulsating, charming and lyrical.

Again the Vicar strode up to the door and gave the knocker three good wraps. The same young woman came to greet us, and again, graciously bid us to come in.

She had on a festive skirt and a head band of matching colors. "There's a slight rehearsal going on in the Common Room. Mr. Anderson said I was to entertain you for a few minutes. Can I offer you a soft drink" she said, spreading her arms wide to include the two of us. "I would like a soft drink, yes!" said the Vicar. "Me too" I added.

While she prepared the drinks, I kept looking out of the window and down the road we had come up that looked desolate now! "With no lights out there on the road, I hope that Doctor Richards can find his way" I said. I was beginning to worry that he wouldn't make it!

"I think we'll be alright! These folks are peace loving people . . . and it's not as if we weren't invited!" she said.

The young lady brought the drinks to us. I looked at it suspiciously. "What kind of drink is this" I asked.

"It's sorrel . . . an old West Indian drink that my mother and grandmother used to make . . . before they moved to New Orleans. I hope you like it!" she said, winning us over with her pleasant way. It was delicious as she said. I drank it slowly, still keeping my eyes on the road outside.

My impulse told me to turn to the Vicar. Suddenly, without warning, her legs buckled, and she fell and hit her head on the edge of the table. I panicked and rushed to her side. She was unconscious with a huge lump on her forehead. "Connie . . . Connie are you alright" I yelled!? I looked up on the table at her glass and I noticed a residue of white powder at the bottom of the glass. Then, it felt like the sky was falling. My own legs began to buckle and dizziness set in.

It was minutes later. I didn't know how long I was out, but when I came to, I was in the large room. There was a majestic looking chair in the middle . . . a huge fire burned in the fire place and the young woman was holding a very large snake . . . half of which slithered up onto her naked shoulders . . . it tasted the air with its forked tongue, while she held its head in her hands.

There was loud singing and the beating of drums. My hands and feet were bound with silk cord . . . several women kept running up to me, snatching the end of my cassock then running back into the small crowd . . . it was clear that they were taunting me.

Part of me was terrified . . . another part of me was holding out . . . I needed to find out where the Vicar was . . . where Huck was! It wouldn't be long until Doctor Richards arrived . . . he'd surely bring the Constable with him.

Like a carnival act . . . through a puff of smoke . . . arrayed in turban on his head . . . ostrich feathers and a long rainbow iridescent cloak came the man of the hour . . . Jilkes Anderson. He came over to me, knelt down, took one hand, grabbed me by the jaw, squeezed hard, and grinned at me.

"Well . . . well . . . well . . . lookee here! If it taint the priest man! Hello dere Priest man. I'm glad you accept my invitation! Memba I told you I was gonna have me own ritual for you . . . well you bout to see me sing and dance . . . jus for you! Hahahaha!" he said. He sauntered calmly over to a darkened corner. He turned and held the limp frame of a little boy over his head!

I began to cough and choke on the smoke in the room! Then my panic became real as I saw the face of the child . . . bound and he was and unconscious. Gilkes put him in the chair and turned triumphantly holding his stick in the air and laughing. There was no doubt . . . it was Huck! Fury suddenly replaced fear in me.

"You hurt that boy and I'll kill you" I roared, struggling against my bonds!

In a move that stunned me, he ran over and walloped me with his cane a couple of times . . . my body felt like it was going into shock in the aftermath of the pain.

He knelt again beside me and grabbed the arm he had hit. "Do you know why I don't let them put a gag on ya mouth!?

Well, it's because I want to here ya pray, Mr. Priest. I want to hear ya scream an pray . . . jus to see if dem words come out! Ha ha ha . . . I bet they don't. Dat would solve the problem, ya know . . . if you could pray. But ya aint got it in ya do ya! You just a bunch of phoney baloney" he said.

Suddenly, I was not afraid. He had made me so mad that I would have fought him if my hands were untied. Instead I called his bluff.

"If you come close to my lips, I will try to say the prayer" I said! He leaned close and sneered at me. I spit in his face! "That's a prayer that doesn't need to be spoken" I said defiantly . . . sneering right back at him.

Gilkes Anderson, jumped to his feet, wiped his face off and laughed. "I'll give it to you . . . you got some guts after all!" he said.

He began to twirl his stick in the air and all around him began to chant! He then made three shrilling sounds, held his arms up in the direction of the skylight! The drumming stopped and all was silent! What looked like a wormhole . . . similar to the one I had seem in the hospital bathroom, appeared in the skylight! Someone or something was entering the room . . . something dark, odious, and mysterious. At first it billowed like a dark cloud . . . descending in silence. It covered the chair until I could no longer see Huck. I panicked and started yelling out his name, "Huck . . . Huck can you hear me! I won't let them hurt you" I said.

Just then, the dark cloud cleared . . . there standing with his black robes shining and his white gloves glowing was Dr. Richards! He was Wippanini! I KNEW IT . . . I KNEW IT ALL THE TIME . . . FROM THE FIRST DAY AT GREENIDGE . . . I SHOULD NEVER HAVE TRUSTED THAT SON OF A . . . ."

My blood coursed through my head and I could feel my veins stretching to the limit in my neck. It wasn't fear of him this time that was making me react this way . . . but sheer hatred of him. It all focused right in on him who had kept me enslaved to fear since my childhood. I had to do something . . . anything to save Huck . . . even if it cost me my life! Then the sinister Richards spoke.

"You can't believe your eyes, can you!? Oh yes . . . it's me Dr. Richards . . . or shall I say The Whip man!?"

"I knew it was you from the start . . . my gut told me it was you!" I yelled out!

"Again you were taken in! That day when you went to sleep on that bench, at that very moment, I took Richards! Oh yes, he was ready you know! The doctors told him he had three corroded arteries and would die without an operation! Fool that he was, he chose not to be operated on! What a convenience for me . . . to be there just when he did . . . to be there to collect two souls!"

His skin was pasty white and it made his hair look odd! He had long elegant fingers with which he stroke Huck's face and neck . . . all the while looking straight at me.

"Let's talk Whip Man. What will it take to let the boy go free?" I said.

"Do you really want to know?" said The Whip Man.

"Yes!" I said boldly.

"Good . . . then take his beating!?" he said.

"What?" Suddenly the young woman with the snake came up to the chair and placed the snake on Huck. It hissed and showed its venomous fangs.

"Take his beating" he said almost in a whisper! "You see, this boy should have been dead a long time ago. He fell off that church roof five years ago and broke his neck. He was miraculously saved somehow. I got there too late to collect my bounty! The only way I'll give him up now, is to take you in his place" he said, still stroking the child as if he were a pet animal.

I looked around to see if there was anyone . . . anyone at all who could save Huck. The assemblage did indeed look like zombies . . . with no will of their own.

"Alright the, take me" I said forcefully. The Whip Man's face grew even brighter. "You don't know how long I've waited for you! You have escaped me for the last time. Now that you have consented, I'll set the boy free!"

As he spoke the words and instantly, Huck's eyes opened. Jumping out of Whip Man's lap and ran over to me, putting his arms again around my neck! "Don't let them hurt me . . . please" he said!

"I won't my boy . . . trust me I won't" I said.

I knew in my mind the extent of the danger I was in, but it didn't matter anymore. I felt like I had the heart of a lion . . . if Whip Man kept his word, Huck would forever be safe!

"Bring me my whip" he shouted! Gilkes came slowly up to him! He bowed and placed the dark whip with the razor blade at the end, which sparkled each time the light from the fire place illumined it.

Gilkes Anderson had three husky men come from the crowd . . . and ordered them to lay me down before The Whip Man. Now I thought of how surreal all this was . . . how my life had been so intricately and delicately intertwined with others who, at other times and situations, took my place in death! This Whip Man was no illusion, he was death . . . come to claim me as his prize.

I heard the whip crack over my head. I began to squirm and wiggle, but the men held me fast. I was resigned to my fate when I turned my head and I saw a woman moving through the crowd unnoticed. She came to the edge of a row of women and stuck her head out! I thought I was hallucinating, but there was my Aunt . . . with that unmistakable head rag on her head.

"You betta pray yo lil. Ass off boy! Don let the Devil take yo' praise . . . it's all ya got! You know how . . . youse a praying man . . .

always have been. Git back to what God made ya for!" she said. As quickly as she appeared, she was gone!

I turned to the side again to see The Whip Man raise his whip over my head. With the grace of God which only comes to the penitent and martyrs, I closed my eyes and said.

"Dear God . . . dear God . . . don't let this be. Forgive the times I let you and my church down! I am not worthy of your forgiveness, nor your love! But through you Son, you redeem me and cancel out my sin. Save now O lord . . . Save me now!"

From across the room Gilkes shouted, "He's praying . . . git the tape and put it cross his mouth!"

Then the singing began again . . . this time it was not those gathered around the chair, but voices streaming into the room from the worm hole above The Whip Man's head. He looked up quickly. Before he could strike a blow, a huge man fell from the hole, glowing like a star! It landed on Whip Man, and disarmed him! One wave of his hand in Gilkes direction broke the cane in half and pinned Gilkes to the floor! The others stepped back against the walls as if they were frightened to death!

For the longest time, there was a silence that was holy in the room . . . this magnificent creature, with the face of a man, glowed like the sun! Huck buried his head in my bosom.

"Don't be afraid said the man! I've not come to hurt you but to free you. God has heard your prayer!" he said.

He left The Whip Man, who was face down on the floor, and came over to me. With another wave of his hand my bonds fell off. I looked into his brilliant face. "I know you" I said, completely in awe of him. "Yes you do" he said!

"You're . . . you're the bellhop from the hotel!" I said. His face was full of peace and he turned to Huck who had his face still buried in my chest.

"Hello Huck . . . remember me" he said softly? Huck turned slowly towards him. The growing smile on his face said it all. "You were that man who helped me when I fell!" With a childlike acceptance, he grabbed the creature around its shoulders and hugged him.

At that moment sirens began to screech outside the building. Blue lights flickered and car doors opened and shut rapidly. The brilliant being turned back to me and spoke softly.

"I must leave now. You will be safe "he said.

"But what about the Whip Man" I said.

"He will be going back with me . . . but be mindful of this . . . he will return someday to get you! This is the way of God!" he said.

"Why did I escape those other times" I asked.

"Simply said, I was in the crib and in the car where you should have been! You can thank you good auntie for God's grace."

"How did you find me tonight?"

"Through a prayer . . . your prayer . . . and through your willing sacrifice and selflessness! You did hear me when I said, 'Suffer the little children' after all . . . in that you did rather well"!

I looked down at Huck. I ran my fingers rapidly through his hair. He smiled at me like a child smiling at his father.

"Do you want to come to America and live there with me"

"Are you going to be my Dad!" he said.

"I'm gonna try" I said.

"Then yes" he said.

We looked toward the ceiling again . . . the funnel was closing as the glorified person ascended in it.

Poking his head around into the room, Mr. Bottoms waved his arm and four constables entered and took charge of the people! Bottoms knelt by my side, "I was told to keep an eye on you!" He held me firmly by a shoulder and patted the boy's head. I was happy to see him and his men. But there was some unfinished business.

"Mr. Bottoms, do you see this man here . . ." I said.

"What man" he said with a puzzled look on his face.

"No matter" I said, holding Huck close.

"We had a look in the locked pantry outside . . . we found the Vicar thrust up into a bundle with her mouth taped" he said. I felt instant panic run through me.

"She . . . she's alright isn't she" I said in a frantic tone of voice.

"Oh yes . . . she'll survive. Though she's gonna be nursing a terrific bump on her forehead for awhile.

CHAPTER 16

It was late evening. In the serenity of the vicarage the Vicar and I stood mesmerized by the cracking hot timbers burning in the fireplace. Although we said not a word, we both realized how very close we had come to danger that night!

"Can I fix you a cocktail" she said in a warm voice.

"I'd like that" I said.

Into her kitchen she went, her heels banging rhythmically against the tiles. In a flash she was back with the drinks.

"I'm a gin and tonic person myself, so I took the liberty of making you one as well. Do you mind" she said, her voice now more sultry?

"Not at all . . . it's my favorite as well" I said.

"I put Huck to bed in the upstairs room. There's a guest room right next to his. I thought . . . maybe . . . maybe you might want to spend the night as well!" She took a sip of her drink then placed the ice cold glass against the bump on her forehead and looked at me.

"Thank you, that's very kind of you" I said.

We went back to staring into the fire . . . it seemed the safe thing to do. She then became pensive. "Didn't you have a clue that Richards wasn't authentic? I mean, I smelled a rat right from the start . . . although I felt it wasn't my place to tell you that. I didn't want to poison you mind against your doctor!" she said.

"Oh yes, I had clues! That very first day in the Gardens at Greenidge! I should have let the smell of flowers be my guide! But circumstances being what they were . . . I mean my sickness and the hospital stay, I just thought I was being paranoid. I really got suspicious when he suddenly excused himself tonight. Then of course there was the feeling of green apples in my stomach!"

"Green apples" she said inquisitively.

"It's a long story. I'll tell you some evening . . . over dinner. You don't find it forward to be asked out by a fellow clergy do you"?

I began to blush slightly! Even I could hear a bit of a flirt in my voice! She smiled back at me. "I don't know! Are you asking me out?" she said in a seductive tone of voice.

"Well yes . . . I guess I am!" I said boldly.

"Like I said before, you should engage life while you have it. So . . . engage me" she said. Her mouth crinkled a bit and it was cute! I needed some excuse right about then to keep myself from being unprofessional.

"I think I'll go upstairs and look in on Huck before retiring!" I said.

"You'll find him just at the end of the hall . . . to the left" she said.

I ascended the staircase slowly, saying a prayer of thanksgiving to God for his having spared my life again. Closing my eyes and facing the wall, I gave silent confession of my sins . . . known and unknown . . . deeds done and left undone.

In the solemnity of the hallway, I acknowledged that I had not been true to my profession. I had the trappings of priesthood, but not the temperament! Like the Levite Priest riding by the man who was robbed and beaten, I paid more attention to acting like a priest than being one . . . for all such sins I truly repented . . . GIVE ME A CLEAN HEART O GOD . . . AND RENEW A RIGHT SPIRIT WITHIN ME!

I went up to the door at the end of the hall and knocked gently. I walked in and, in the dark; I could see the outline of a great canopy bed. I tipped toed up to the bed, so as not to wake him.

"Huck . . . Huck are you still awake" I whispered.

"There was no response. I pulled the curtain back and there, standing on the other side of the bed looking at me, was the

Heavenly One and a little brown faced boy, in a garment of pure light. Shocked momentarily, I closed my eyes, clasp my hands together and knelt before them.

"Don't be afraid, we won't hurt you"! I stood up slowly, keeping my head bowed! "I'm not afraid! Where is Huck" I said?

"Here . . . right next to me!" said the Heavenly One!

"That . . . that's Huck" I said in disbelief.

"Meet him who was your kinsman in life . . . his name is Huck Anderson . . . son of Gilkes and Rosey Anderson" he said.

"You mean . . . this is . . . this is . . ."

"Yes, the child who took your place in death!" With unsteady steps, I walked around the bed to where they stood. I knelt again, this time before the boy! He looked at me through loving eyes . . . eyes that perfectly resembled Huck's eyes.

"May I ask whose heavenly presence I am in" I said!

"I am Penile, ambassador of the Most High and guardian of all children. I'm here to take Huck home. The Whip Man took him a long time ago . . . his coming back has fulfilled the purpose for which he was sent to help you grow into the priest God always meant you to be . . . to help you to realize that you too are mortal and must die someday . . . but . . . not today!" My mind was reeling with the knowledge that I was really talking to a divine messenger . . . I was in the presence of the divine and It humbled me . . . my mouth was dry!

"It was you wasn't it? . . . that little white boy who called me to action in front of St. Marks Church that day so many years ago?" I said.

"Yes" said the Heavenly One.

The boy came up to me and put his hand in mine. Thank you for the ice cream . . . it was a sweet as the love you bore Huck!"

"We will leave now!" said Peniel. "You will see me again, when I come to restore you to The Father" he said.

The wormhole appeared behind them. As they turned and went into it, I could hear a heavenly song being sung. Then suddenly all was quiet and I was left in the darkened room alone.

The only thing I could think to say was "Thank you for your mercy Lord"! I turned to go out the door. It was then that I smelled it . . . the clear scent of flowers! I looked cautiously behind me and into the darkened corners of the room . . . there was nothing there! The feeling of green apples in my stomach was gone. It never did come back!

The End